GREYHOUND COMMANDER

GREYHOUND COMMANDER

CONFEDERATE GENERAL
John G. Walker's
History of the CIVIL WAR
West of the Mississippi

EDITED BY RICHARD LOWE

Louisiana State University Press

Baton Rouge

Published by Louisiana State University Press
Copyright © 2013 by Louisiana State University Press
All rights reserved
Manufactured in the United States of America
First printing

Designer: Laura Roubique Gleason
Typeface: Ingeborg
Printer and binder: Maple Press

Maps created by Alexander Mendoza

LIBRARY OF CONGRESS CATALOGING-IN-PUBLICATION DATA
Walker, John George, 1822–1893.
 Greyhound commander : Confederate General John G. Walker's history of the Civil War west of the Mississippi / edited by Richard Lowe.
  pages cm.
 Includes bibliographical references and index.
 ISBN 978-0-8071-5250-8 (cloth : alk. paper) — ISBN 978-0-8071-5251-5 (pdf) — ISBN 978-0-8071-5252-2 (epub) — ISBN 978-0-8071-5253-9 (mobi) 1. Southwest, Old—History—Civil War, 1861–1865—Campaigns. 2. Southwest, Old—History—Civil War, 1861–1865—Personal narratives, Confederate. 3. Walker, John George, 1822–1893. 4. Generals—Confederate States of America—Biography. I. Lowe, Richard G., 1942– II. Title.
 E470.9.C34 2014
 973.70976—dc23

2013007862

Contents

Maps

Editor's Preface

While doing research in the 1990s for a history of John G. Walker's Texas Division in the American Civil War, I came upon a document that had been examined by previous researchers but was not widely known among non-specialists in the war west of the Mississippi River. General Walker himself, shortly after the conflict ended, had written a history of the war in the Trans-Mississippi Department. Considering that Confederate generals in that region left few—arguably, only one—published memoirs of their wartime experiences, Walker's history seemed a good candidate for publication to a wider audience.

The general's account, dictated to one of his daughters while his family lived in London in 1866–67, covered the war west of the Mississippi River from the outset of hostilities to the late spring of 1864. Walker had evidently intended to carry the story down to the end of the American conflict in 1865, but his return to the United States in 1867 and his heavy involvement in a long string of business ventures apparently intervened, and the narrative ended with the last day of the Red River Campaign in May 1864.

A family member, Myron Gwinner of Tulsa, Oklahoma, later donated the history to the rich collections at the United States Military History Institute in Carlisle Barracks, Pennsylvania, where it now resides in the Myron Gwinner Collection of Civil War documents. Mr. Gwinner's family generously made the manuscript available to all researchers and put no restrictions on publication. Thus, nearly 150 years after it was written, General Walker's history is presented to scholars and general readers interested in the man himself and in the Civil War in Arkansas, Louisiana, and Texas.

As editor, I have generally left the text alone, wishing to preserve the account as cleanly and as close to its original form as possible. Words that were clearly misspelled have been included as originally written unless the misspelling could create ambiguity or confusion in the minds of readers. The general's organization of the long story into chapters has likewise been retained. The habit of the general (or his daughter, who typed up the narrative) of using "it's" to mean the possessive "its" is not accompanied by a long string of "[sic]" notations. Instead, I have changed "it's" to "its" where appropriate. Obvious typographical errors have been corrected. Inconsistent spelling of certain words (especially "volunteer") has been left as in the original. Walker often reeled off long sentences of complex structure—so complex in some cases that I have added a comma or some other editorial aid in brackets to clarify his meaning. I have identified people, places, and events mentioned in the history to give it context and meaning for a later audience, and I have pointed out those errors of fact that crept into the narrative. The result, I hope, is an account that stands on its own and does not require long training in the history of the Civil War to appreciate and understand.

As every author admits (at least to himself), the final product of a long research project is the result of the knowledge and kindness of many people who helped along the way. Myron Gwinner of Tulsa, Oklahoma, deserves thanks for making the manuscript available to the public at the U.S. Army Military History Institute. The unparalleled master of the Civil War collections at that great archive, Richard J. Sommers, introduced me to the Walker history as well as numerous related collections for my work on Walker and his men. Joan M. Wood, an archivist in the Stewart Bell Jr. Archives in the Handley Regional Library of Winchester, Virginia, was very efficient in tracking down documents about Walker's family life. James McGhee of Jefferson City, Missouri, who knows more about Confederate military units in Missouri than anyone else, guided me to sources on the war in his state. Four generous colleagues—the late Arthur W. Bergeron Jr., of Carlisle Barracks, the leading specialist on Louisiana Confederate units and related topics; Steven Mayeux of Cottonport, Louisiana, the expert on the war in central Louisiana; Carl Moneyhon of the University of Arkansas at Little Rock, an authority on the mid-nineteenth century in both Arkansas and Texas; and Daniel Sutherland of the University of Arkansas, author of numerous major works on the Civil War—all helped me in various ways, but especially in understanding navigation on Arkansas and Louisiana rivers during the Civil War era.

Brad Clampitt of East Central University in Oklahoma provided valuable documents on the postwar pardon of General Walker. Gary D. Joiner of Louisiana State University at Shreveport, author of two books on the Red River Campaign, guided me to the archaeological findings on the U.S. Navy's ironclad ship, the *Eastport,* buried for nearly 150 years in the mud of the Red River. Debbie Reulet of St. Joseph Plantation in Vacherie, Louisiana, explained the mysteries of the physical properties of "coolers" on Louisiana sugar plantations. Bob Hufford of Hopewell, Virginia, provided biographical information on some rather obscure Confederate officers. My colleagues at the University of North Texas, Randolph B. Campbell and Richard B. McCaslin, read an early draft of the introduction and ironed out some infelicities and glitches. Another colleague, William Kamman, guided me through the thicket of State Department records in the National Archives.

I dedicate the book to three fine men—Kevin, Chris, and Mark Lowe—because they are my sons and think highly of me. I dedicate it also to my wife, Kathy, who read early drafts and took on extra tasks to allow me to work for long stretches without interruption (except by three inconsiderate dogs).

GREYHOUND COMMANDER

The General and His History

When Walt Whitman wrote in 1882 that "the real war will never get in the books," he could not have known that, over the next century, fifty thousand books on the American Civil War would be published. And in the following thirty years, thousands more volumes, examining and dissecting the war down to the tiniest detail and from almost every conceivable angle, have poured out of the publishing houses. In addition to new biographies, battle studies, political surveys, and the usual stew of subjects, historians have produced books on syphilis and funeral practices, post-traumatic stress disorder and the war's effects on families. Now, with university and commercial presses rumbling and clacking under the weight of the sesquicentennial of the war, readers may expect many more titles on everything from Father Abraham and Marse Robert to the sources of morale, from analyses of sound to conceptions of the human body. Whitman was America's great poet of the mid-nineteenth century, but he was not much of a prophet.[1]

It seems at times that historians and interested readers have examined every possible Civil War subject—several times over. True, the profession and the reading public could possibly survive a year or two without another study of Gettysburg or another examination of Abraham Lincoln, but not all facets of the war have been so heavily analyzed. The war west of the Appalachians, although much better understood today than ever before, still has stories to tell and lessons to teach. The war west of the Mississippi River is no longer "forgotten" or ignored, but historians still have heavy work to do on the trans-Mississippi theater as well. Although armies and campaigns and battles were smaller in this westernmost region, they did affect the larger war and are therefore worthy of further examination. Moreover, readers and scholars interested in the experiences of common soldiers will find that near starvation was just as traumatic in Louisiana, Arkansas, and

Missouri as in Tennessee or Virginia. Camp life was equally boring, sleeping on the cold ground was just as bone-chilling, marching barefoot was as painful, wasting away from dysentery or measles was as wretched, and dying was as final.

One feature of the war west of the great river that is still relatively underdeveloped is the view from the generals' tents. Unlike Confederate generals in the eastern and western theaters of operations, those in the trans-Mississippi wrote (or published) very little about their own experiences and opinions in the war. Readers interested in personal accounts by Confederate generals in the East have long been familiar with the memoirs and reminiscences of men like Edward Porter Alexander, P. G. T. Beauregard, Jubal Early, John B. Gordon, Josiah Gorgas, James Longstreet, and other luminaries of the conflict in Virginia, Maryland, and Pennsylvania. High-ranking Confederate generals in the western theater who produced valuable first-hand accounts of the war west of the Appalachians included Basil Duke, John Bell Hood, Joseph E. Johnston, St. John Richardson Liddell, and Dabney H. Maury.

By contrast, high-ranking generals in the Trans-Mississippi Department (that is, those who commanded districts, armies, and divisions) produced very few first-hand accounts of the war. Short sections of the books by Liddell and Maury (each of whom served for a time west of the river) should of course be mentioned here, and an unpublished diary by Camille Armand Jules Marie, Prince de Polignac (better known as "General Polecat" to his Texas soldiers), does exist. But only one full-blown published memoir by a leading Confederate general—a book comparable to some of the best by anyone, Union or Confederate—has been available to students of the war in the trans-Mississippi region: Richard Taylor's *Destruction and Reconstruction* (1879). Taylor's flair with a pen, his joy and dazzling talent in verbal combat, his sharp wit, and his mastery of British and American literature make this book a delight to read, even 130 years later. He provides sharp and revealing sketches of politicians and fellow officers and leaves no uncertainty about his judgments of men he found lacking, especially Nathaniel P. Banks and Edmund Kirby Smith. Scholars and other students of the Civil War understand the conflict west of the river more clearly because of Taylor's book.[2]

Although Taylor's superb memoir stands almost alone, one other prominent Confederate major general did write a history of the war west of the Mississippi River. Unpublished until now, this account by the commander of "Walker's Texas Division," John G. Walker, is important for a number of reasons. First, it is now one of only two full-scale published chronicles by leading Confederate generals in the westernmost theater of the American Civil War. Second, Walker wrote his history shortly after the war, while his memories were still fresh and vivid. In addition, although Walker's judgments of men and events often mirrored those of Taylor, and although the two men cooperated closely in 1863–64, the commander of "Walker's Greyhounds" did interpret some parts of the story differently, occasionally disagreeing directly with Taylor. Finally, of course, General Walker and his infantry division played a prominent role in the conflict in Arkansas, Louisiana, and Texas; he provided a critical angle of view for later students of the war; and he recounted some events known only to him.

So, who was John George Walker, and how did he come to write this account? He was born into a prominent middle-class southern family in 1821 in Howard County, central Missouri, on the left bank of the Missouri River.³ When he was a young boy, his father's farm household included eight white family members, two slaves, and two free African Americans, indicating a thriving family of above-average means. Howard County was populated primarily by migrants from the Upper South and was part of a section of the state that later became known as "Little Dixie" because of its southern-born population and pro-southern sympathies during the Civil War.⁴

Many of Walker's forebears and kinsmen achieved some prominence in public affairs. His paternal grandfather, George Walker, was the colonel of the Prince Edward Militia in Virginia during the Revolution and served as an aide on George Washington's staff. Various uncles and cousins served as United States senators, attorney general of Kentucky, chief justice in Arkansas, and governor of Florida. Another cousin (Alexander Stuart Walker) became an associate justice of the Texas Supreme Court in the 1880s. The general's father, John, born in Virginia, married a niece of Andrew Jackson in Tennessee and later moved his family to central

Missouri in 1818. He was elected to the state senate as a Democrat in 1828 and served as the fourth state treasurer of Missouri, from 1833 to 1838. Young George (as his mother and sisters called him) lived for several years with his family in the building in Jefferson City (the state capital) that housed the state treasury as well as the family's quarters, only three blocks from the state capitol and governor's mansion. The future Confederate general, then, grew up in a prosperous, educated, and well-known family with a strong tradition of public service, a history as small slaveholders, attachments to "Little Dixie," and an allegiance to the Democratic party.[5]

When he reached his late teens, Walker's family bundled him off, down the Missouri River, to St. Louis to study at the Jesuit College (now Saint Louis University) in the heart of the city (now the location of the city's convention center). The Jesuit priests and other staff members were evidently efficient instructors, for Walker became an articulate and cultivated adult who wrote clearly and efficiently, appreciated the art and history of Europe and the Middle East, and was well informed on the public issues of his day. If he had not become a soldier, he might have become successful in any number of other pursuits—the law or politics or commerce, for example—because he was well equipped intellectually to succeed in mid-nineteenth-century America. In May 1846 at age twenty-four, with no military training but probably with the help of his family's influence, he secured an appointment as a first lieutenant in a new regular-army regiment of mounted riflemen raised to defend the Oregon country in the far Northwest. The war between Mexico and the United States intervened, however, and Colonel Persifor Smith's Mounted Rifle Regiment was redirected to the Southwest to join tens of thousands of newly enlisted and excited volunteers on their way to Mexico.[6]

The new lieutenant, it turned out, had an aptitude for war. His regiment was part of General Winfield Scott's army on the march from Veracruz, on the Gulf of Mexico, to Mexico City in 1847. On that victorious 250-mile march, Walker won high praise from his superiors. The Americans were harassed and bothered continually along the road to Mexico City by "relentless, partisan 'rancheros.' It was hard riding nearly all the time, encounters almost daily," according to one veteran of the regiment. When the army paused at Puebla, about two-thirds of the way to Mexico City that summer, Mexican soldiers and partisans continued their raids on the edges of the U.S. encampments and ambushed unwary detachments from the main body. On July 30, fifty miles northeast of the city of Puebla, Walker's detachment from the Mounted Rifles struck back. According to Captain C. F. Ruff, with only 82 men the Americans drove off 200 Mexican foot soldiers and 100 horsemen in three hours of hard house-to-house fighting and destroyed "a large quantity of valuable military supplies." Captain Ruff and Colonel Persifor Smith noted Walker's "gallant and meritorious" conduct in this encounter and recommended him for a brevet promotion to captain, which was eventually granted.[7]

Brevet Captain Walker continued to impress his superiors when Scott's army reached the vicinity of Mexico City in the late summer. At the Battle of Molina del Rey on September 8, the Mounted Riflemen, led by Walker and Ruff, "charged under heavy fire, encountered an impassable ravine which they turned, and defeated a vastly superior force," according to the historian of their regiment, who witnessed the fight. Walker was slightly wounded during the engagement, but he recovered quickly enough to fight five days later in the dramatic battle that captured Chapultepec Castle on the outskirts of Mexico City. Once the castle fell, the Mounted Riflemen pursued defending Mexican troops to the Belén gate into the city itself. Here, Walker was wounded a second time. His regiment, among the first to enter the city the next morning, raised the American flag over the National Palace in the main plaza and formed an honor guard to escort Winfield Scott into the plaza.[8]

The Mounted Riflemen remained in Mexico nearly a year after the war and returned to Jefferson Barracks, the largest army post west of the Mississippi River, eleven miles downriver from St. Louis, in late July 1848. After several months of training and reorganization, the regiment turned again to its original assignment, protection of the migrants traveling to the Oregon country, 2,500 road miles away. Walker thus began a dozen years of service on the western frontier, from Jefferson Barracks to Fort Leavenworth in Kansas to Oregon, down to California, back to Leavenworth, and eventually to the rugged western fringes of settlement in Texas and New Mexico (including part of what is now Arizona).[9]

During those years the captain was sometimes lonely, some-times flushed with adrenalin in military action against various Indian tribes, and sometimes more like a tourist or travel writer than a soldier. On the route to Oregon, Walker wrote his mother back in Jefferson City that he had been "cut off from all commu-nication with the world for nearly four months." Indeed, he joked, "we are altogether 'behind the times here,' [and] our latest news from 'the settlements' [i.e., the settled portion of the country]" was already two months old. Another officer in the regiment recalled later that the wilderness between Kansas and Oregon was "a coun-try without roads, often without wood water, or grass." In fact, he continued, "excepting Fort Kearny in Nebraska and a fur trading post at Laramie in Wyoming there was not a house between Leav-enworth and the Columbia River [in Oregon]." Routine duty in the dark wet forests of Oregon was certainly different from the adven-tures that had thrilled Walker in Mexico.[10]

Not all was tedium for the young officer, however. Sometime after the regiment returned to Fort Leavenworth in July 1851, Walker, now a regular captain rather than brevet, was granted a leave of absence, of which he took full advantage by sailing to Eu-rope to travel the continent and the eastern Mediterranean as a tourist. Like a modern sightseer who crams as many locales and experiences as possible into a limited amount of time, Walker vis-ited London, Paris, Lyons, Marseille, Genoa, Pisa, Florence, and Rome—all in May and June 1853. Somewhere on his itinerary, he joined and traveled with U.S. Senator Stephen A. Douglas of Il-linois, another good Democrat, who was sampling the sights and sounds of Europe. After Rome, Walker set out to see Naples, Malta, Egypt, "the Holy Land," Constantinople, and Trieste in July and August. Although he was dazzled by the art, architecture, and fes-tivals of Rome and found that St. Peter's Basilica "exceeds my wild-est dreams in its magnificence," he wrote his sisters that "our own Country is a thousand years ahead of the best Country in Europe." He was repelled by the class divisions in England, military despo-tism in France, and the "superstition & intolerance" of the Catholic Church in Italy. One may well doubt that he found Cairo or Con-stantinople closer to his notion of a great society.[11]

When Walker returned from his European adventure, he joined

his regiment (now renamed the First Regiment of Mounted Riflemen and later designated the Third U.S. Cavalry) at Fort Inge on the southern end of the Texas frontier. In August 1854 he wrote his sisters in Jefferson City that "I have generally been very busy hunting Indians, etc. but have enjoyed excellent health notwithstanding the hot weather." The young captain had some violent scrapes with the Lipan Apache in southwest Texas, demonstrating again his initiative and dependability under fire. Most of the regiment, including Walker, was reassigned to New Mexico in 1856 to deal with unhappy tribes in the southern Rocky Mountains.[12]

At about the same time he was ordered to New Mexico, Walker married Melissa Smith, about whom little is known. Whether the marriage was broken by death or some other cause is uncertain, but two years later, he married Sophie M. Baylor in New Orleans, a cousin on his father's side of the family. Sister of the well-known Virginia novelist, essayist, and poet, Frances Courtenay Baylor, and daughter of a U.S. Army officer, Sophie also had ties to Texas. Two uncles (John R. Baylor and George Wythe Baylor) were prominent Indian fighters, secessionists, and, later, Confederate officers in the Lone Star State. Her literary sister and her mother eventually moved in with Sophie and spent the war and postwar years living and traveling with the Walkers. Nine children were born to the Walker family, but two infant sons died during the Civil War and an infant daughter died shortly after the conflict.[13]

While he was stationed in New Mexico, Captain Walker had another opportunity to travel through exotic regions and record his impressions, but this time his observations were official. The army sent him on two exploring expeditions into what is now northeastern Arizona in the summer of 1859 to report on the Navajo Indians and the natural features of the region. On his first journey Walker was either the first or one of the first white Americans to see the wonders of Canyon de Chelly, an ancient home of southwestern pueblo-dwelling Indians, occupied for thousands of years until abandoned 150 years before Columbus reached the New World. Walker's expressive prose was put to good use in his description of "the novel and beautiful sight of a waterfall of nearly a thousand feet in perpendicular height, from the tableland above to the bottom of the cañon. The volume of water was considerable, but after falling some hundreds of feet it was broken into a lace-like sheet of pure white which swayed back and forth with the wind; a little further down it became spray and finally reached the bottom as fine mist."[14]

The man who had readily fought the Apache in Texas was not mere aggression and belligerence. He could imagine himself in the situations of the Navajo bands he found on his exploration, and he recognized that some of the Native Americans were no danger to others. One poor group in Canyon de Chelly, he reported, "seem very unwarlike and well disposed towards us, but upon them the chief burden of war with us would fall, for the destruction of their growing corn would reduce them to starvation and extreme misery." Indeed, he concluded, "a war made upon [the Navajos] by us would fall heaviest upon the least guilty—would transform a nation which has already made considerable progress in civilized arts into a race of beggars, vagabonds and robbers. . . . it may be that some little forbearance [by the United States] might be the part of true wisdom." His empathy for the Indians did not extend to Mormon settlers in the West, however. He referred to them as "fanatics" who encouraged Indians to attack American settlers: "should a war break out between our troops and the tribes I believe it will have been brought about in no inconsiderable degree by Mormon influence and intrigue."[15]

Walker's few surviving letters from the 1850s provide little evidence that he was caught up in the sectional strife then gripping the nation. Still, he was a native of "Little Dixie" in central Missouri, his family had been small slaveholders when he was a youth, and some of his uncles and cousins and in-laws were outspoken defenders of "southern rights," so his sympathies and associations inclined him toward the southern cause. When the war finally broke out in the spring of 1861, the captain was stationed at Fort Union in northeastern New Mexico. He resigned his commission in the U.S. Army in July 1861 and accepted a commission as a major of cavalry in the Confederate Army in early August. What had been a happy and successful career in the U.S. Army thus ended abruptly, and Walker's life turned in a new direction.[16]

He spent the first year and a half of the war serving in the main

Confederate Army in the East, the famed Army of Northern Virginia as it was eventually known. In its urgent search for experienced and talented military men, the Confederacy found Major Walker almost immediately and promoted him to colonel with command of a brigade in September 1861. Only four months later, based partly on his efficient leadership of his brigade during the fall, he was promoted again, to brigadier general, with command of North Carolina, Virginia, and Arkansas regiments. His quick promotions, from major to colonel to brigadier general, were evidently sponsored by a superior officer who would help him move up the ranks in the army and shape his entire Confederate career, Major General Theophilus H. Holmes. Already in his late fifties by the time the Civil War began, Holmes had been a classmate of Robert E. Lee at the U.S. Military Academy (class of 1829). He had been cited for gallant service in the Mexican War and had just recently been promoted to major general in the Confederate Army in October 1861. Holmes apparently considered Walker an officer with great abilities and much potential and gave him increasingly important duties to perform from late 1861 to late 1862.[17]

Walker's first significant action in his new rank was during the Federal Peninsula Campaign in the late spring and summer of 1862. During the initial stages of this massive drive toward the Confederate capital of Richmond, Walker's brigade was stationed on the fringes of the fighting, guarding the water approach to Richmond at Drewry's Bluff, about ten miles south of the capital city on the James River. Ordered to reinforce the main Confederate body on the outskirts of Richmond in late June, the brigade did not come under fire until the last engagement of the Seven Days Battle, Malvern Hill, on July 1. General Holmes, commander of the division that included Walker's brigade, took position on the extreme right of the Confederate line, next to the James River. Holmes was not a man to dash forward without excellent reasons, and his brigades eventually stood still and engaged in an artillery duel with Federal guns on Malvern Hill and U.S. Navy gunboats on the river. The naval barrage was particularly effective, according to the report from Walker's brigade: the gunboats kept up "an incessant fire with guns of the heaviest caliber with extraordinary precision." Firing from both sides faded away with the diminishing daylight, and the men returned to Drewry's Bluff the next day.[18]

General Walker's reactions to the battle, if he ever recorded any, have not survived, so we cannot know what lessons he drew from this engagement. Two observations he may have made involved artillery and infantry. Walker and his men were perhaps fortunate to have so cautious a commander in this particular engagement. Elsewhere on the battlefield, thousands of Confederates, commanded by more aggressive leaders, marched up Malvern Hill and were easily cut down by Federal artillery. The Confederate army lost more than five thousand men that day, most of them to the concentrated Federal artillery on Malvern Hill. Massed artillery with clear lines of fire could devastate the most determined infantry. In addition, naval guns—almost always heavier and more destructive than the light fieldpieces of infantry—were particularly dangerous to foot soldiers on open ground. Walker may well have had flashes of memory of Malvern Hill later in the war, when his commands were ordered by his superiors to advance across open ground against Federal artillery and U.S. Navy gunboats and ironclad ships.

Soon after Malvern Hill, Walker was given control of two more brigades and thus became a division commander. His was one of four divisions left near Richmond after the Seven Days to keep an eye on the Federals while the rest of the main Confederate Army dashed north to fend off other advances by Union generals at Cedar Mountain and Manassas. Thus, General Walker missed the battles at those two locations and would not hear hostile fire again until the Antietam campaign in September 1862.[19]

When the main body of Robert E. Lee's Army of Northern Virginia marched into western Maryland in September, Walker's new division was operating with Thomas Jonathan (Stonewall) Jackson's wing of the army. Jackson was assigned to capture the Federal strongpoint at Harpers Ferry, Virginia, where the Shenandoah River empties into the Potomac, about fifty straight-line miles northwest of Washington, D.C. Walker's brigades were assigned by Jackson to occupy Loudoun Heights, directly across the Shenandoah River east of the town of Harpers Ferry. This high ground was particularly valuable because Walker's artillery could drop shot and shell into Federal positions in the town, but the Confederate gunners were nearly invulnerable to counter fire because their position was so elevated. Another Confederate division set up artillery positions across the Potomac River, on Maryland Heights. Meanwhile, Jackson's infantry and field guns pressed the Federals from the west. When the artillery under Walker and other Confederate units rained iron and lead down on the defenders on September 15, it was soon obvious that Harpers Ferry could not be held. The resulting capitulation of nearly twelve thousand Federal soldiers, the largest surrender of U.S. Army forces until World War II, allowed Jackson's wing to rush north to join the rest of Lee's army at Sharpsburg, about seventeen miles away in western Maryland.[20]

Two days after the fight at Harpers Ferry, Walker's division was in the thick of the Battle of Antietam (called the Battle of Sharpsburg by most Confederates), the bloodiest day in American history. Initially stationed on the far right of the Confederate line, Walker's brigades were summoned by General Lee around mid-morning to move rapidly to the left to shore up the Confederate defense, under a fierce assault by superior numbers. Racing along the rear of Lee's entire line, Walker's men reached the threatened left wing around 10 a.m. Their general whipped his column into line of battle at the hottest point of contact and helped to stem the Federal advance. After the peril from the left died away, more Federal divisions aimed new hammer blows at the Confederate center, and Walker turned part of his division to face the new threat. For a time, only four Confederate cannon and a few hundred men stood between the advancing enemy and victory. Indeed, one of Walker's regiments, the Twenty-seventh North Carolina Infantry, stood "boldly in line without a cartridge," in the admiring words of General Lee. Thus, bits and pieces of the Confederate infantry, including part of Walker's division, again shored up the wobbly and outnumbered Confederates. Once more the gray line bent backward but held, and the Federal advance slowed to a halt. Walker's exhausted and bloodied soldiers did not participate in the third and final assault of the day, on the Confederate right at a bridge across Antietam Creek. Instead, the men dropped to the ground and rested where they had fought earlier in the day. When the sun finally set on the gory farm fields around Sharpsburg, the two armies were roughly where they had been when the sun rose that morning.[21]

Walker's reputation in Lee's army as a dependable, hard-nosed, fighting general was made in the three days from Harpers Ferry to Sharpsburg. His efficient use of artillery at Harpers Ferry contributed significantly to the surrender of the Federal garrison. The rapid movement and quick deployment of his division in the vortex of the fight on the Confederate left at Antietam was noted by many observers, including Generals Lee and Longstreet. Lee's report on the battle mentioned the timely arrival of Walker's brigades to reinforce the shaky gray line: it was "relieved by Walker's command, who immediately attacked the enemy vigorously, driving him back with great slaughter." Longstreet noted the dash to buttress the Confederate center later that day: "the forces of Generals Jackson and Walker came to our relief." Indeed, he wrote, at one point "our center was extremely weak, being defended by but part of Walker's division and four pieces of artillery." The noted historian of Lee's generals, Douglas Southall Freeman, concluded that the men of Walker's division "had acquitted themselves most honorably." Here, surely, was a general who would prove valuable to the Army of Northern Virginia.[22]

General Walker was doubtless proud of his officers and men, and although no written reaction to the campaign has survived among his papers, he must have looked forward to another promotion and increased responsibility within Lee's army. In the heat of the action at Sharpsburg, he had conferred personally and cooperated with the most important leaders of the army—Lee, Longstreet, and Jackson—and they had given him his due in their reports. After the army's return from Maryland, General Lee gave his division important tasks and trusted in Walker's ability to operate independently. His future in the Army of Northern Virginia seemed to hold great promise.

And then—to the surprise of General Lee and probably Walker himself—he was transferred to the faraway theater of war west of the Mississippi River in early November. The region across the river was sometimes the destination of officers who had failed to perform adequately in the East. Generals John B. Magruder and

Theophilus H. Holmes were recent examples. But Walker had excelled, not failed, and his transfer was a disappointment to General Lee. The army commander wrote President Jefferson Davis that his army would be less effective without the services of Walker and two other officers who were being transferred to other theaters. "I feel that I am much weakened by the loss of [men like Walker], but I hope the general service will be benefited." Some generals in U.S. military history would have stormed and fumed and demanded the retention of able subordinates. (George Patton in World War II comes to mind.) But Lee's basic politeness and deference produced only the pointed phrase, "I hope the general service will be benefited."[23]

No direct and explicit explanation for Walker's transfer is provided in his own papers, in the records of President Jefferson Davis, or in the *Official Records* of the war, but the reason was probably Theophilus H. Holmes. The older general had taken Walker under his wing in late 1861, approved his promotions, and praised his abilities to others. When Holmes was reassigned to the trans-Mississippi theater shortly after the Seven Days in July 1862, he doubtless wished to have a proven officer like Walker under his command. The fact that Holmes was a personal friend of President Jefferson Davis would have given a request for Walker's transfer considerable weight in the executive mansion. In any event, on November 11 Walker was ordered to report to General Holmes in Little Rock, Arkansas. If he was disappointed in leaving the Army of Northern Virginia—and no evidence exists on that point—his simultaneous promotion to major general probably lightened his steps to the west.[24]

Walker arrived in Little Rock on December 13, 1862, and was quickly given command of a new and untested infantry division made up of Texas regiments and batteries. In fact, it was the only division on either side in the Civil War to consist throughout its existence of units from a single state. The new major general took command of the Texans on New Year's Day 1863. On a bitterly cold and windy afternoon, a few miles south of Little Rock, the Texans were drawn up at dress parade to receive their new commander, riding from regiment to regiment on an iron-gray horse and addressing the troops in small groups. One observant private described Walker as "a small man, weight about 140 lbs., . . . auburn hair, very large blue eyes, long bunch of beard upon his chin, and a mustache; in all a handsome man." Walker would lead this division in all its engagements with the enemy and remain with it until the last few months of the war, when he was assigned to command the Confederate District of West Louisiana.[25]

Trans-Mississippi Theater

Walker spent his first few months with the Texans marching and countermarching across southern Arkansas and northern Louisiana, following the orders of superiors who were confused about where the U.S. Army presented the greatest threat: Trans-Mississippi Confederate headquarters in Shreveport and the rich

Red River Valley of northwest Louisiana, or the fortified city of Vicksburg on the Mississippi River across from northeast Louisiana. After a great deal of marching and steamboating back and forth between one supposed target and the other, the Texas division faced fire for the first time in late May and early June 1863. In a futile attempt to relieve pressure on Vicksburg, then under siege by U. S. Grant's army, Walker's superiors ordered his division to attack three Federal posts along the west bank of the Mississippi River, a short distance upriver from Vicksburg. The Confederate high command in Shreveport hoped to cut Grant's supply line along the right bank of the river and thereby force him to suspend operations against Vicksburg in order to restore his communications. In the interim, they hoped, the besieged Confederate army in the river city would have a chance to escape the encircling enemy.[26]

General Walker knew this to be a hopeless task because he had learned that the Federal Army had already abandoned the supply line on the west side of the river in favor of a new route on the opposite shore, out of reach of the Confederates. Nevertheless, he followed his orders and, working directly under Major General Richard Taylor, commander of the District of West Louisiana, sent his three brigades to assault the enemy outposts. Two of the advances were basically stillborn for one reason or another, but the attack on the Federal camp at Milliken's Bend, Louisiana, turned into a bloody hand-to-hand struggle on the river's levee. The Texans managed to maul the defenders into a retreat from the levee back to the riverbank, but the arrival of naval gunboats and furious shelling of the seemingly victorious Confederates ashore eventually sent the Texans scrambling back out of range, leaving the two forces essentially where they had begun the day.

The Battle of Milliken's Bend made no tactical difference in the Vicksburg campaign or in the war because the Confederate objective was already out of reach, but the fight was important for at least two other reasons. First, the Texas division got its first taste of combat. Two of the brigades did not come to grips with the enemy, but the Texans at Milliken's Bend had experienced not only the emotional extremes and exhilaration of deadly close-in fighting, but also disturbing post-battle emotions, especially those men who witnessed the bloody scenes around a field hospital in the rear and the burial of comrades. Second, Milliken's Bend was one of the earliest demonstrations of the war (preceded only by the siege of Port Hudson near Baton Rouge a few days earlier) that black Americans, armed and ably led, could fight as hard and as desperately as any men. General Walker understood from this encounter the great threat that African American soldiers presented to Confederate arms.

The division spent the next several weeks roaming along the west bank of the Mississippi River, burning farms and plantations that had been taken over by northern entrepreneurs after the owners had fled. Walker's men were then ordered to central Louisiana in the vicinity of Alexandria to blunt any new enemy thrusts up the Red River toward Shreveport or overland toward Texas. The feared enemy advance moved from New Orleans in October 1863, up through southern Louisiana, stalled near the town of Opelousas about sixty miles south of Alexandria, and then began a slow retreat southward. A few regiments of one of Walker's brigades, joined by two thousand gray cavalry, attacked the Federal rear guard at Bayou Bourbeau a few miles south of Opelousas in November 1863. The nearly two thousand Federals, veterans of the recent Vicksburg campaign, were caught completely off guard by the Confederate infantry and were quickly routed and sent on a rapid sprint to the rear, with Confederate horsemen whooping on their heels. Reinforcements from the main Federal body hurried back to the rear and put a stop to the embarrassing skedaddle. General Taylor, unimpressed by the earlier failures along the Mississippi River, congratulated Walker on the conduct of his Texans. Their performance "has responded to [my] highest hopes and expectations. They pressed the veterans of Vicksburg with a coolness, resolution, and perseverance that was irresistible."[27]

After spending the winter of 1863–64 harassing and interrupting enemy traffic on the Mississippi River, Walker's division was drawn into the largest operation of the war in the Trans-Mississippi: the Red River Campaign in the spring of 1864. In order to include Louisiana in President Lincoln's Reconstruction plan, to destroy Confederate headquarters and shops in Shreveport, to gather up mountains of Louisiana and Texas cotton for idle New

England textile mills, and to warn the French away from their adventures in Mexico, the Federal high command organized a three-army simultaneous movement on Shreveport. General Nathaniel P. Banks would lead the largest force overland, up from New Orleans to Alexandria, where he would unite with part of the Federal army that had steamed down from Vicksburg. Together the two components would drive up the Red River and meet a third Federal army, marching south from Little Rock, Arkansas. Their rendezvous at the gates of Shreveport, they believed, would force the Confederate high command in the Trans-Mississippi Department to abandon its headquarters and production facilities in and around Shreveport or fight against overwhelming odds. Once Shreveport had fallen, the door to East Texas, untouched by war, would be opened for Federal occupation.

Federal armies began rumbling toward their destinations in March 1864, and the overmatched Confederates scrambled to put together some sort of defense. Although the entire defensive campaign was legally under the command of Confederate authorities in Shreveport, the highest-ranking officer actually facing Banks's army in the field was Richard Taylor. He called on friendly regiments and brigades from scattered areas around Louisiana, Texas, and Arkansas to gather along the Red River as quickly as possible and join him in the defense of the Red River Valley. At the core of the small army he commanded for most of the campaign was Walker's Texans. Taylor led the Greyhound division, a smaller division of Louisiana and Texas troops under Alfred Mouton, and miscellaneous cavalry companies and artillery batteries on a slow retrograde movement up the Red River, waiting for more units to arrive from Texas and Arkansas before he would have the strength to strike at the enemy.

Although he was still greatly outnumbered, once Taylor was joined by horse brigades from Texas in early April, he prepared to stand his ground. He found a suitable spot on April 8 about forty miles south of Shreveport, near the small town of Mansfield, and waited for Banks's Federals to emerge onto open ground from a single road through a thickly wooded approach. Before Federal officers could fully prepare for an all-out assault by the Confederates, Taylor unleashed his infantry, hoping to drive the enemy back into the woods, where the clogged country road would prevent any sort of orderly retreat. General Mouton's division, the left wing of Taylor's army, moved first, then General Walker's Texas division, the right wing, began the long run across open ground against Federal artillery and infantry. Taylor had caught Banks before the latter could fully deploy his army, and the Confederates, despite heavy fire, overran Federal infantry and artillery and sent them streaming back into the woods in disorder. The only road through the forest was jammed with Federal supply wagons, many abandoned at the approach of the onrushing attackers, and the battle turned into a rout.

In the Battle of Mansfield (called Sabine Crossroads by the Federals), Walker's division performed at a very high level. The Texans rushed forward in good order, continued to move across open ground despite suffering significant casualties, and shattered the left wing of the Federal army, capturing an entire battery with all its appurtenances, hundreds of prisoners, thousands of small arms, and scores of supply wagons. After darkness finally ended the fighting in the woods, the Greyhounds dropped to the ground, exhausted, and slept for only a few hours before they were sent in pursuit of Banks's retreating army the next morning. On April 9 General Banks deployed his entire army along the roads and fields near the small town of Pleasant Hill, twenty miles south of the previous day's battle. Believing that the Federal will to resist was broken by its defeat at Mansfield, Taylor sent his infantry across open ground again at Pleasant Hill to finish the previous day's work. This time, though, he was facing the full force of the Federal army, and a mistake by Confederates on the right end of the Confederate line enabled veteran Federal units from Vicksburg to sweep down a slope into the Confederate flank, sending the newly arrived Arkansas and Missouri units into a disorderly retreat. Walker's Texans on the left were sent forward by Taylor once the battle had begun, again across open fields toward an enemy waiting for them. The Greyhounds ran forward, swept completely around some Federal units, and forced others to retreat in the failing light. Joined by allied horsemen and the exhausted division of General Mouton, Walker's men pushed the Federal line back into the town of Pleasant Hill, when darkness created confusion on both sides and prevented further pursuit. The Confederate failure and re-treat on the right was balanced by the success and advance on the left, but the two armies essentially fought to a standoff. General Walker received a painful wound to the groin during the battle and was sent to the rear by Taylor, but Walker's Texans had fought like veterans and earned praise from the enemy and from General Taylor. In Taylor's estimation, Walker's division had become the heart of his army.

After General Banks began the long retreat from Pleasant Hill to Alexandria far down the Red River, the Confederate high com-mand turned its attention to the third Federal army, the one from Little Rock that was supposed to press Shreveport from the north. Edmund Kirby Smith, commander of the entire Trans-Mississippi Department, to the dismay and disbelief of Generals Taylor and Walker, detached most of Taylor's units from his command and left the victor of Mansfield with only a few thousand men to pur-sue Banks's army of nearly thirty thousand toward Alexandria. Smith had decided to lead the bulk of Taylor's army plus Confeder-ate cavalry in Arkansas—ten thousand men altogether—north to turn back the blue column from Little Rock. Taylor, placing great confidence in Walker and his Texans, believed he could damage Banks severely if Walker's division was part of the chase, but de-spite vehement remonstrance from Taylor, Smith insisted on his own plan and kept Walker's division under his command for a new campaign in Arkansas.

The Federal army from Little Rock had bogged down on its way to Shreveport and had taken up a defensive posture at Camden in south-central Arkansas. When the Union commander, Fred-erick Steele, realized that Banks's defeated army was retreating away from Shreveport and that a sizeable Confederate army was approaching Camden, he decided to abandon the town and hurry back to Little Rock and safety. For four days in late April, Smith's Confederates pursued Steele's Federals north of Camden. The skies had been pouring torrents of rain on the countryside for days, and both armies had to pull themselves through deep mud. The Con-federates caught up to Steele on the banks of a river swollen out of its normal bounds, the Saline, at a crossing known as Jenkins' Ferry, about fifty miles south of Little Rock, on April 30. The soldiers fought each other in what was practically a swamp for several hours. At times the splashing of water by hundreds of men drowned out the shouts of their officers, and the soldiers had to guess what they were supposed to do. Steele had selected a strong defensive position that forced the Confederates, hemmed in by streams and swamps to left and right, to attack straight across watery open fields.

Walker's Texans were the last to throw themselves against the Federal line after Arkansas and Missouri regiments had been forced back. This time, there was no dramatic sweep across open ground and pursuit of a fleeing enemy. The Texans splashed and slogged through the ankle- and knee-deep water straight at the Federals firing from behind log breastworks. Charge and countercharge resulted in no real progress, however, and Steele's men held their line. All three of Walker's brigade commanders were wounded in the melee, two fatally, and the Texans began to mill around and lose cohesion. In the end, the Federals managed to stave off the attackers long enough to cross a pontoon bridge over the river at their backs and then destroy the pontoons to prevent pursuit. Steele had avoided a complete disaster, but he had also failed to pressure or capture Shreveport, and the Confederates could claim a strategic victory even if the Federals claimed tactical success in the Saline swamp.

Now that Kirby Smith had removed any possibility of a threat on Shreveport from the north, he agreed to release the infantry that Taylor had pleaded for before pursuing Banks's army down the Red River in Louisiana. After a few days' rest, the Texas Greyhounds were put on the road and asked to race to Taylor's side somewhere around Alexandria, more than three hundred miles to the south. Worn out from long marches and three pitched battles in one month, the men nevertheless lined up in thinned ranks for the next leg of their seemingly endless journey. General Taylor, harassing Banks's army on its retreat, anxiously looked for signs of Walker's arrival. "Like 'Sister Ann' from her watch tower, day after day we strained our eyes to see the dust of our approaching comrades. . . . Not a camp follower among us but knew that the arrival of our men from the North would give us the great prize in sight." Despite their reputation as greyhounds, the Texans could not reach Taylor until late May, five days after Banks had escaped down the river toward New Orleans. Taylor was furious that he had been deprived of Walker's brigades until too late, and he blamed Kirby Smith for Banks's escape.[28]

General Taylor placed no blame on Walker and his men, though. They "held every position entrusted to them, carried every position in their front, and displayed a constancy and valor worthy of the Guards at Inkermann or Lee's veterans in the Wilderness!" Taylor wrote in his memoir. He might have been even more impressed if he had calculated the movement of the Greyhounds since the start of the Red River Campaign in mid-March. In seventy days the Texans had marched, sometimes without food or tents, 930 miles and fought three significant battles. It was one of the more amazing physical achievements by any body of men in the entire war.[29]

Taylor's anger toward Kirby Smith boiled over after the Red River Campaign. The angry letters the two generals sent flying at each other eventually led Confederate President Jefferson Davis to separate the two antagonists by reassigning Taylor to an important command east of the Mississippi River. That appointment left a vacancy in the headquarters of the District of West Louisiana, and Kirby Smith appointed General Walker to succeed Taylor in command of the district in June 1864. The hard-bitten Texans said farewell to their popular commander in an emotional ceremony near Alexandria. Deeply disappointed in his reassignment, they recalled that he had led them through every fight they had ever had, that he had done his best to provide for them, and that he had always been in the thick of the action with them, not directing affairs from the rear.

Indeed, Walker had become wildly popular with his men. Captain H. A. Wallace of the Nineteenth Texas Infantry wrote his wife that "our whole Army loves Gen Walker. he is the best Gen. On this side of the Miss. [S]ure treats his men best." Colonel Wilburn King of the Eighteenth Texas Infantry was happy to serve under Walker, whom he regarded as "an excellent soldier and one of long experience." Douglas French Forrest, a Confederate naval officer stranded by the fortunes of war in Galveston, offered his services to Walker as a staff officer and had a chance to observe him from close range. Walker, he wrote, "is the most popular General in the

Trans Mississippi & has acquired his popularity by gallant service in the field & an equal & regular, but very rigid discipline." A voluble Irishman in the division, Joseph P. Blessington, remembered later that Walker's "presence was always hailed with the wildest enthusiasm by both officers and soldiers." Even newspapers in Alabama and South Carolina, in printing reports of affairs west of the Mississippi, noted that Walker enjoyed "unbounded popularity with his men." In the last few weeks of the war, Forrest wrote that Walker's Texans "have clamored so loudly for their old General that [his successor, John H.] Forney[,] has been relieved from the command & it has been tendered to Walker to whom they are warmly attached." The trust and affection between the general and his foot soldiers doubtless contributed significantly to their success.[30]

In his new office in Alexandria, General Walker dived into the details and administrative tangles that command of a large district entailed. Manpower shortages, supply bottlenecks, angry civilians, foot-dragging subordinates, smuggling, mail delivery, courts martial—the challenges seemed endless. After only two months in that position, Kirby Smith appointed Walker to command the District of Texas, New Mexico, and Arizona, with headquarters in Houston. The same types of administrative duties and problems he had wrestled with in Louisiana were of course present next door in Texas as well, and Walker again moved quickly and directly to work. He continued in these duties for several months until the spring of 1865, when Kirby Smith, fearful of another Federal attack on Texas and determined to have a proven combat officer on the scene, appointed him to lead Tom Green's old cavalry corps.[31]

That assignment was brief, however, and in early May, by popular demand of the men in his old infantry division, the general was returned to the command of the Greyhounds, then marking time near Hempstead, Texas, sixty miles northwest of Houston. By then, all Confederate armies east of the Mississippi River had surrendered, and the common-sense Texans, realizing that victory was now impossible, did not wait for formal surrender ceremonies. Instead, without orders and despite the pleas of their officers, they simply packed up their few possessions and walked away from their camps, counting the miles before they reached home. Some of them, resentful that they had apparently wasted three years of their lives, often with no pay, decided to even the scales by raiding the army's quartermaster and commissary stores for food, mules, wagons, and whatever else would compensate them for their troubles. The lack of a formal surrender and the illegal property seizures by some of the men made for an anticlimactic end to the Greyhound division.[32]

Shortly after the breakup of the Trans-Mississippi army, Walker and a small party of colleagues, believing from reports in northern newspapers they would be prosecuted for treason if they remained in the United States, left their last duty post in Houston and traveled down to Mexico. From there, Walker sailed to Havana, Cuba, and then London, where he established a household for his wife, her sister, her mother, and several of his children. By late 1866 Walker was hopeful that he could return to the United States without danger of harsh reprisals from the federal government, and he applied for an individual pardon from President Andrew Johnson. Walker appealed to several U.S. Army officers and other government officials for letters of support. The U.S. Minister to France, former Major General John A. Dix, told President Johnson that Walker "was humane to our prisoners during the war, and always conducted himself like an honorable enemy." Another Union general, Gordon Granger, wrote that he had known Walker for twenty years and assured Johnson that he was "a man of the highest integrity & great moral worth." After some bureaucratic dead ends and inconvenient delays, the pardon was granted, Walker took the required oath of allegiance in March 1867, and he brought his extended family back to the United States shortly afterward. Traveling with the Walkers was an English nurse, or nanny, indicating that the family's life was comfortable by the standards of the day.[33]

Even before he left London, Walker began a long business career that allowed him to support his family in some comfort. In 1866 he was a director and English agent of a Virginia company that promoted Confederate settlement and mining in Venezuela. He was at the same time a partner in a New York firm established to sell railroad iron and machinery in the southern states and to market southern crops in England. At some point in 1867, he returned to the United States and settled his family in Jefferson, Texas, in the northeastern corner of the state. He must have been an aggressive and successful businessman because he continued to take advantage of new opportunities in the late 1860s and 1870s. In 1869 he was a Texas agent for a St. Louis life insurance company. Meanwhile, as an officer of the Houston & Texas Central Railway, he arranged for three hundred Chinese workers from California to build a westward extension of the rail line, the same type of work Chinese immigrants provided to the first transcontinental railroad at about the same time. While the former general traveled frequently in pursuit of his business affairs, his family lived first in Jefferson, then moved to New Orleans in the early 1870s. At some point in the mid-1870s, they moved again, this time to his mother-in-law's hometown of Winchester, Virginia. From this time forward, the Walker family called Winchester home.[34]

In the early 1870s he was associated with three different newspapers in Dallas and Austin and was an editor and proprietor of the *Austin Democratic Statesman* (now known as the *Austin American-Statesman*). He soon returned to a job he knew something about: promoting immigration to Texas, this time as an officer of the Texas & Pacific Railway. Like several of his other postwar positions, this one involved extensive travel, but it also included something new—lobbying for favorable laws in the Texas and national legislatures. In May 1875 he became a board member and vice-president of a Dallas newspaper (later known for many decades as the *Dallas Times-Herald*). Life was not all business for Walker, though. He joined veterans' organizations, supported old colleagues in their public disputes about wartime events, and generally kept alive the memory of his service in both the U.S. and Confederate armies.[35]

The former general's antebellum and wartime military association with men who would become prominent political and business leaders after the war helped catapult him into affairs of the federal government in the late 1880s. President Grover Cleveland, the first Democratic president since before the Civil War, appointed Walker as United States consul in Bogotá, Colombia, in 1887. One of the new consul's comrades in the old Mounted Rifles, Dabney H. Maury, was U.S. minister to Colombia and doubtless supported Walker's appointment. In his memoirs Maury spoke very highly of Walker's personal character in the old army before the Civil War. Certainly, Maury worked closely with Walker and left the ministry in his hands when he (Maury) was away. President Cleveland also appointed him as a special envoy to the Latin American republics to invite them to the first Pan-American Conference, in Washington, D.C., in 1889–90. For a man who worried that he might be prosecuted for treason by the U.S. government a quarter-century earlier, Walker had come a long way.[36]

By the early 1890s Walker was in his early seventies. He had been healthy since childhood and was active in business and government affairs throughout his postwar life. Two days before his seventy-second birthday, on July 20, 1893, he was talking with a friend in Lafayette Square, directly in front of the White House in Washington, when a sudden paralysis seized him, probably the result of a stroke. Despite the ministrations of friends and physicians, the Missouri soldier, businessman, and diplomat died later the same day. His body was taken to Winchester, where he had resided with his wife and daughters and in-laws in the family home, Elmwood. An honor guard of Union and Confederate army officers met his casket when it arrived at the train station. At his funeral in Christ Episcopal Church on July 22, his bier was covered with evergreens offered by Federal officers and Confederate colors provided by former comrades. The mourners accompanied his body to a plot he had chosen for his burial in Mt. Hebron Cemetery, and the leader of the Texas Greyhounds was laid to rest on the morning of his birthday. He was survived by many of his old foot soldiers, who, to their own dying days, proudly reminded willing listeners that they had marched with Walker's Texas Division.[37]

How did the general come to write his history of the war in the Trans-Mississippi Department? While living in England immediately after the war and waiting for word that it would be safe to return to the United States, the general decided to record his own history of the war west of the river from 1863 to 1865, while his memory was still fresh. According to one family tradition, he dictated his account to one of his daughters, who later typed her father's words for easier reading. Some additional words and small corrections are scattered through the typescript in the general's handwriting, so it is clear that he tried to be as accurate and detailed as possible.[38]

Walker's account of the war in the Trans-Mississippi Department was packed with facts and historical information. His narrative, especially when he wrote about events he knew about only second-hand, of course could not be as full or accurate as it might have been had he written it later, when more documentary evidence was available and when wartime passions had cooled somewhat. Thus, his narrative of events in Missouri early in the war, while he was far away on his journey from New Mexico to Virginia, reveal his southern bias. In his accounts of events he had witnessed, though, Walker was fair and usually accurate. He had little patience for northern politicians, but he could not help but respect his old home, the U.S. Army. He normally gave full credit to the accomplishments of the officers and men in blue. Like other southern officers, he found the idea of black soldiers in Union uniforms repellent, but he was quick to realize the great potential that black regiments held for Federal military success.

Like his district commander, Richard Taylor, Walker came to hold the abilities of Edmund Kirby Smith, commander of the Trans-Mississippi Department, in very low regard. Smith's refusal to allow Walker to join the rest of Taylor's small army in pursuit of Nathaniel P. Banks's defeated Federals at the end of the Red River Campaign in 1864 was particularly wrong-headed in Walker's view, and he blamed Smith for Banks's clean escape. Generals Walker and Taylor usually saw military affairs in the same light, and they had obvious respect for each other, but Walker criticized his commander for some of his decisions. For example, the two men clashed briefly after the Battle of Milliken's Bend in 1863, when Taylor, in Walker's opinion, unfairly criticized his Texas troops for flinching under heavy naval fire. In addition, Walker believed Taylor put too much faith in fortifications and river obstructions at Fort De Russy early in the Red River Campaign. Still, the two men, both veterans of the war in Virginia, cooperated closely and effectively when they fought together in the Trans-Mississippi theater.

Walker's history provides a valuable look at the problems Confederate commanders grappled with in the Trans-Mississippi Department. Physical separation from the war east of the river in 1863 and later made cross-river military coordination extremely difficult. The long delays in communication and the scarcity of news from Mississippi, for example, made intelligent planning for relief of Vicksburg impossible. When the Confederate government attempted to cross his division over the river to shore up Confederate defenses in the last year of the war, Walker was chagrined to learn that many of his Texans simply refused to cross the Mississippi. The river had become a mental as well as physical barrier, and hundreds of Texans either left the ranks without permission (although most returned voluntarily) or threatened to do so rather than leave their families without a military shield.

Confederate officers in the Trans-Mississippi were also required to cover great distances with relatively few troops in order to defend the region. Combat in the Eastern Theater of the war stretched from Gettysburg, Pennsylvania, on the north to Appomattox, Virginia, on the south, a distance of about 190 miles. Walker's men ranged as far south as Carencro, Louisiana, and as far north as Austin, Arkansas, about 325 miles, and they usually traveled over worse roads than those in Virginia, Maryland, and Pennsylvania. Armies in the Eastern and Western theaters often included 50,000 or more men (sometimes more than 100,000), but Walker's Division of about 5,000 sometimes fought independently and was never part of any army larger than 10,000. Compared to the horrific bloodletting in the battles in the East, those in the western area were much less destructive. Although the Greyhounds suffered significant losses during the war (2,175 casualties), nearly 40 percent of their number in 1864, the gaps in their ranks were smaller than those in many divisions east of the Mississippi. Some of Lee's divisions dwindled down to mere regimental size during the same period.

Fewer men, greater distances, less direction or aid from the Confederate capital, smaller battles—all these features of the war

west of the river made the conflict very different from the struggle
Walker had seen in Virginia and Maryland. Nevertheless, the campaigns in the Trans-Mississippi influenced Federal troop disposi-
tions in other theaters and thereby shaped the war in Tennessee,
Georgia, the Carolinas, and Virginia. The Red River Campaign,
for example, probably lengthened the war by months by diverting
troops meant for Union armies in Georgia and allowing the Confederates to reinforce the opposing gray columns north of Atlanta.
Moreover, for those researchers and readers interested in the "bottom up" view of the war—the war as experienced by the men in the
ranks—the Trans-Mississippi theater provides that angle of view
as much as any other. The war west of the river, although clearly
different from the hostilities farther east, deserves study if all the
moving pieces of the military puzzle are to be understood. General
Walker's history contributes to such an understanding.

NOTES

1. Walt Whitman, "Specimen Days," in *Complete Prose Works* (Philadelphia:
David McKay, Publisher, 1892), 80. In 1988 the historian James M. McPherson
noted that more than fifty thousand books about the Civil War had been published and that the war was the most written-about event in the nation's history
(*Battle Cry of Freedom: The Civil War Era* [New York: Oxford University Press,
1988], ix).

2. Richard Taylor, *Destruction and Reconstruction: Personal Experiences of
the Late War* (1879; rpt. with an introduction by T. Michael Parrish, New York:
Da Capo Press, 1995). For Liddell and Maury, see Nathaniel C. Hughes, ed., *Liddell's Record* (Dayton, Ohio: Morningside House, Inc., 1985); Dabney Herndon
Maury, *Recollections of a Virginian in the Mexican, Indian, and Civil Wars* (New
York: C. Scribner's Sons, 1894). Microfilm copies of Polignac's unpublished diary
of his service in the Trans-Mississippi Department are at various repositories in
the United States, including the U.S. Army Military History Institute.

3. Some biographical sketches list Walker's birth as July 22, 1822, but the
headstone on his grave in Mt. Hebron Cemetery in Winchester, Virginia, and a
handwritten genealogical list in his papers give the year as 1821. Some sketches
also identify Cole County, Missouri, as his birthplace, but the same genealogical
list specifies Howard County. See John G. Walker Genealogy and Letters, Myron
Gwinner Collection, U.S. Army Military History Institute, Carlisle Barracks, Pa.

4. Fifth Census of the United States, 1830, Records of the Bureau of the Census, Record Group 29, National Archives, Washington, D.C., Howard County,

Missouri (Microfilm M19: roll 73, p. 146); Robert M. Crisler, "Missouri's Little Dixie," *Missouri Historical Review* 42 (January 1948): 130–39.

5. John G. Walker obituary, *Washington Post,* July 21, 1893; Sons of the American Revolution Membership Applications, 1889–1970, on-line database, image 590 (Provo, Utah: Ancestry.com Operations, Inc., 2011), search.ancestry.com/search/db.aspx?dbid=2204 (accessed July 10, 2011); Walker's obituary in *Winchester* (Va.) *Times,* August 2, 1893; "Alexander Stuart Walker," in Tyler et al., eds., *The New Handbook of Texas* (Austin: Texas State Historical Assn., 1996), vol. 6: 792; Missouri State Treasurer, www.treasurer.mo.gov/History/JohnWalker.aspx (accessed January 12, 2012).

6. *Washington Post,* July 21, 1893 (obituary); Saint Louis University, www.slu.edu/sluhistory/timeline.html (accessed January 14, 2012). J. G. Walker to Dear Mother, March 30, 1849; J. G. Walker to My Dear Sisters, March 23, 1853; J.G.W. to My dear Sisters, July 1, 1853; [John] George [Walker] to My Dear Sisters, August 17, 1854, all in Walker Genealogy and Letters, Myron Gwinner Collection (examples of Walker's prose and appreciation for European and Middle Eastern art and history). Ralph C. Deibert, *A History of the Third United States Cavalry* [originally Persifor Smith's Mounted Rifles] (Harrisburg, Pa.: Telegraph Press, 1933), 2–6.

7. C. F. Ruff to James B. Bowlin, November 1, 1848, C. F. Ruff Papers, Missouri Historical Museum, St. Louis; Charles Morton, "Third Regiment of Cavalry," in Theo. F. Rodenbough and William L. Haskin, eds., *The Army of the United States: Historical Sketches of Staff and Line with Portraits of Generals-in-Chief* (New York: Maynard, Merrill, & Co., 1896), 196; Deibert, *History of the Third United States Cavalry,* 8. Walker was promoted to full captain (i.e., not brevet) in June 1851. See John G. Walker file, Compiled Service Records of Confederate General and Staff Officers, and Nonregimental Enlisted Men, War Department Collection of Confederate Records, 1825–1900, Record Group 109 (Microfilm M331, p. 2), National Archives (cited hereinafter as Walker file, Compiled Service Records, with appropriate page number).

8. Deibert, *History of the Third United States Cavalry,* iv, 9–10. One of Walker's fellow officers described him as the "gallant J. G. Walker" for his daring and leadership during the assaults near Mexico City. See Morton, "Third Regiment of Cavalry," 197.

9. Deibert, *History of the Third United States Cavalry,* 10, 16–17; Howard R. Lamar, ed., *The New Encyclopedia of the American West* (New Haven, Conn.: Yale University Press, 1998), 871. The distance from St. Louis to Portland, Oregon, via today's modern highways and bridges is more than two thousand miles.

10. J. G. Walker to Dear Mother, March 30, 1849, Walker Genealogy and Letters, Myron Gwinner Collection; Deibert, *History of the Third United States Cavalry,* 16.

11. J.G.W. to My Dear Sisters, July 1, 1853, John G. Walker Papers, Missouri Historical Museum.

12. George to My Dear Sisters, August 17, 1854, Walker Genealogy and Let-

ters, Myron Gwinner Collection; Thomas T. Smith, Jerry D. Thompson, Robert Wooster, and Ben E. Pingenot, eds., *The Reminiscences of Major General Zenas R. Bliss, 1854–1876: From the Texas Frontier to the Civil War and Back Again* (Austin: Texas State Historical Assn., 2007), 105; Maury, *Recollections of a Virginian*, 90; Thomas T. Smith, *The Old Army in Texas: A Research Guide to the U.S. Army in Nineteenth-Century Texas* (Austin: Texas State Historical Assn., 2000), 139; James T. King, *War Eagle: A Life of General Eugene A. Carr* (Lincoln: University of Nebraska Press, 1963), 15–16; obituary in *Winchester* (Va.) *Times,* August 2, 1893; Deibert, *History of the Third United States Cavalry,* 18.

13. Obituary in *Winchester* (Va.) *Times,* August 2, 1893; genealogical sketch in Brookie Benham to Dear Ben, June 28, 1975, in John G. Walker Papers, Stewart Bell Jr. Archives, Winchester-Frederick County Historical Society, Handley Regional Library, Winchester, Va.; Catherine T. Mishler, "Baylor, Frances Courtenay," in John T. Kneebone, J. Jefferson Looney, Brent Tarter, and Sandra Gioia Treadway, eds., *Dictionary of Virginia Biography,* 3 vols. to date (Richmond: Library of Virginia, 1998–), vol. 1: 400–402; Thomas W. Cutrer, "Baylor, George Wythe," in Tyler et al., *New Handbook of Texas* 1: 422–23; Cutrer, "Walker, John George," in Tyler et al., *New Handbook of Texas* 6: 795–96; Jerry Thompson, "Baylor, John Robert," in Tyler et al., *New Handbook of Texas* 1: 423–24.

14. National Park Service brochure on Canyon de Chelly, www.nps.gov/cach/index.htm (accessed January 16, 2012); J. G. Walker and O. L. Shepherd, *The Navajo Reconnaissance: A Military Exploration of the Navajo Country in 1859,* ed. L. R. Bailey (Los Angeles: Westernlore Press, 1964), 41. This book reprints Walker's reports on the two expeditions.

15. Walker and Shepherd, *Navajo Reconnaissance,* 47, 54, 93.

16. Walker file, Compiled Service Records, p. 2. Walker's odyssey from Fort Union to Virginia is recounted in the memoirs of one of his traveling companions. See Maury, *Recollections of a Virginian,* 133–41.

17. Walker file, Compiled Service Records, pp. 3, 5, 8, 11, 15, 17, 19, 48, 61; "Theophilus Hunter Holmes" in Ezra J. Warner, *Generals in Gray: Lives of the Confederate Commanders* (Baton Rouge: Louisiana State University Press, 1959), 141. Holmes told Robert E. Lee in April 1862 that Walker's brigade was one of only two he could count on in the presence of the enemy. See *The War of the Rebellion: A Compilation of the Official Records of the Union and Confederate Armies,* 128 vols. (Washington: Government Printing Office, 1880–1901), ser. 1, vol. 9: 465 (hereinafter cited as *Official Records,* with all citations to series 1).

18. Report of Walker's brigade in *Official Records* 11, pt. 2: 915; *Official Records* 11, pt. 2: 908, 984.

19. *Official Records* 12, pt. 2: 553; John G. Walker, "Jackson's Capture of Harper's Ferry," in Robert Underwood Johnson and Clarence Clough Buel, eds., *Battles and Leaders of the Civil War,* 4 vols. (New York: Century, 1887–88), vol. 2: 604. Walker's account of the action at Harpers Ferry includes details not available elsewhere.

20. *Official Records* 19, pt. 1: 912–14, 958–59; Walker, "Jackson's Capture

of Harper's Ferry," in Johnson and Buel, *Battles and Leaders of the Civil War* 2: 604–11; Douglas Southall Freeman, *Lee's Lieutenants: A Study in Command,* 3 vols. (New York: C. Scribner's Sons, 1942–44), vol. 2: 193–97; Stephen W. Sears, *Landscape Turned Red: The Battle of Antietam* (New York: Ticknor & Fields, 1983), 144.

21. *Official Records* 19, pt. 1: 149, 150 (quotation from Lee's report); *Official Records* 19, pt. 1: 914–21 (reports of Walker and his brigade commanders).

22. *Official Records* 19, pt. 1: 149, 840; Freeman, *Lee's Lieutenants* 2: 270. For indications that Lee had confidence in Walker and planned to use his division in new roles after Antietam, see *Official Records* 19, pt. 2: 675, 676, 680.

23. *Official Records* 19, pt. 2: 697; Walker file, Compiled Service Records, pp. 5, 51, 56. For sketches of Magruder and Holmes, see Peter S. Carmichael, "Magruder, John B., " and Anne J. Bailey, "Holmes, Theophilus H.," in Richard N. Current, ed., *Encyclopedia of the Confederacy,* 4 vols. (New York: Simon & Schuster, 1993), vol. 3: 988–89, and vol. 2: 785.

24. Walker file, Compiled Service Records, p. 51; Bailey, "Holmes, Theophilus H.," in Current, ed., *Encyclopedia of the Confederacy* 2: 785.

25. John C. Porter, "Early Days of Pittsburg, Texas, 1859–1874; 18th Texas Infantry, Company H, Life of John C. Porter and Sketch of His Experiences in the Civil War," p. 10, 18th Texas Infantry file, Historical Research Center, Hill College, Hillsboro, Texas; Walker file, Compiled Service Records, p. 53; Richard Lowe, *Walker's Texas Division, C.S.A.: Greyhounds of the Trans-Mississippi* (Baton Rouge: Louisiana State University Press, 2004), 62; Douglas French Forrest, *Odyssey in Gray: A Diary of Confederate Service, 1863–1865* (Richmond: Virginia State Library, 1979), 306–7.

26. The material in this and following paragraphs that outline Walker's command of the Texas division is based on Lowe, *Walker's Texas Division.*

27. Taylor's congratulations are reprinted in Joseph Palmer Blessington, *The Campaigns of Walker's Texas Division* (1875; rpt., with new introductions by Norman D. Brown and T. Michael Parrish, Austin, Texas: State House Press, 1994), 145. Blessington was a member of the Sixteenth Texas Infantry and the division's first historian.

28. Taylor, *Destruction and Reconstruction,* 188. Taylor's remark about "Sister Ann" referred to a literary folktale ("Bluebeard") in which a woman in distress searched the horizons for signs of a rescue party.

29. Taylor, *Destruction and Reconstruction,* 188.

30. H. A. Wallace to Dear Achsah, February 10, 1864, Harvey Alexander Wallace Papers, Southwest Arkansas Regional Archives, Washington, Ark.; L. David Norris, ed., *With the 18th Texas Infantry: The Autobiography of Wilburn Hill King* (Hillsboro, Texas: Hill College Press, 1996), 68; Forrest, *Odyssey in Gray,* 306–7; Blessington, *Campaigns of Walker's Texas Division,* 72–73; *Charleston* (S. C.) *Mercury,* August 10, 1864.

31. Walker file, Compiled Service Records, 36–39, 55, 60; Cutrer, "Walker, John George," in Tyler et al., *New Handbook of Texas* 6: 795–96.

32. Brad R. Clampitt, "The Breakup: The Collapse of the Confederate Trans-Mississippi Army in Texas, 1865," *Southwestern Historical Quarterly* 108 (April 2005): 498–534; Walker file, Compiled Service Records, 36–39, 55, 60; Cutrer, "Walker, John George," 319.

33. The nanny remained with the household for the rest of her life, and after death her body was buried in the same cemetery with the Walkers (Case Files of Applications from Former Confederates for Presidential Pardons ["Amnesty Papers"], 1865–67, Records of the Adjutant General's Office, 1780s–1917, Record Group 94 [Microfilm M1003, pp. 6, 8, 10–12, 14], National Archives). Walker's route to London is outlined in the memoir of his nephew and recent aide-de-camp, Joseph C. Ralston, in Reminiscences of Joseph Courtney Ralson, typescript in Vanderslice-Ralston Family Papers, in possession of Becky Vanderslice, Boulder, Colo. For the English nurse, see Brookie Benham to Dear Ben, June 28, 1975, and "Other Tombstones—Mt. Hebron Cemetery," both in Vanderslice-Ralston Family Papers.

34. The best brief account of Walker's business affairs is in a biographical sketch by Thomas W. Cutrer in Tyler et al., *New Handbook of Texas* 6: 795–96.

35. Tyler et al., *New Handbook of Texas* 6: 795–96; Richard B. McCaslin, *Fighting Stock: John S. "Rip" Ford of Texas* (Fort Worth, Texas: TCU Press, 2011), 251, 254.

36. Maury, *Recollections of a Virginian,* 58; Dabney H. Maury to Thomas F. Beyard, October 25, 1887, in General Records of the Department of State, 1756–1993, Despatches from U.S. Ministers (Colombia), Record Group 59 (Microfilm T33, reel 41), National Archives; Brown, "John George Walker," in Davis, *Confederate General,* 6: 88–89.

37. Obituary in *Washington Post,* July 21, 1893; "Funeral of Gen. Walker," *Washington Post,* July 21, 1893; obituary in *Winchester Times,* August 2, 1893; Brookie Benham to Dear Ben, June 28, 1975, and "Other Tombstones—Mt. Hebron Cemetery," both in Vanderslice-Ralston Family Papers.

38. The preface to Walker's history was written in his wife's hand not long after his death in 1893. That preface provides a few details about the writing of the account.

THE WAR OF SECESSION
WEST OF THE MISSISSIPPI RIVER
DURING THE YEARS
1863 – 4 – & 5.

BY

John G. Walker.
Major General. C.S.A.

Mrs. Walker's Preface

This partial history of the campaigns of the Trans-Mississippi Department was written by my husband the late ~~Gen.~~ Major-General John G. Walker, C.S.A. in London, England, at the close of the Civil War when the events which he narrates were fresh in his mind, & the feelings which they called forth were uppermost in his thoughts.

For the first two years of the war he fought under Genl Lee in the army of Northern Virginia & was with Stonewall Jackson at the capture of Harper's Ferry occupying Loudoun Heights, & then took part in the battle of Sharpsburg. After this engagement he was promoted to Major Gen & transferred to the Trans-Mississippi Dept, later relieving Genl Taylor in command of the Dept. of La. [District of West Louisiana] where he remained until the close of the [illegible word] from there transferred to the Com. Of the Dept of Texas [District of Texas, New Mexico, and Arizona], where [*sic*]

CHAPTER 1.

[No chapter title]

In order to afford the reader a clearer understanding of the events of the last three years of the war, west of the Mississippi, it will be useful to review briefly the occurrences of 1861 and '62.

Missouri, the most populous of the States west of the Mississippi, although peopled largely by emigration from the slaveholding states of Virginia, North Carolina, Kentucky, and Tennessee, and deeply sympathizing with the people of those states in their war against abolitionism, were yet so strongly attached to the Union that all the efforts of her State Government, thoroughly Secession in its tendencies, was unable to carry the State out of the Union.[1] Her legislature, however, after the formal secession of some of the southern states, fearing the aggressive tendencies of the Federal Government, passed a law for the thorough organization of the state militia,[2] and the Governor [Claiborne Jackson], the constitutional commander in chief of the state forces, immediately took measures to carry the law into effect, by establishing throughout the state encampments for military organization and instruction.[3] A camp of this character was established in the suburbs of St. Louis, called Camp Jackson, under the command of

---

1. Virginia, North Carolina, Kentucky, and Tennessee accounted for 52 percent of all American-born residents of Missouri in 1860. See U.S. Bureau of the Census, *Population of the United States in 1860; Compiled from the Original Returns of the Eighth Census* (Washington: Government Printing Office, 1864), 301.

2. The Military Bill of May 10, 1861, gave the state governor total control of the state militia and required every man in the state to serve (William E. Parrish, *Turbulent Partnership: Missouri and the Union, 1861–1865* [Columbia: University of Missouri Press, 1963], 24, 41).

3. Governor Jackson, thoroughly sympathetic to the southern cause, tried to use the state militia to oust Federal troops from Missouri. See Russell K. Brown, "Jackson, Claiborne Fox," in David S. and Jeanne T. Heidler, eds., *Encyclopedia of the American Civil War: A Political, Social, and Military History* (New York: W. W. Norton & Co., 2000), 1055–56.

Brigadier General [Daniel M.] Frost, a soldier by profession, and formerly an officer in the United States Army.[4]

Entertaining well grounded apprehensions that the ultimate effect of this movement would be to carry the state out of the Union, since the well known sentiments of the State Government, and Legislature were in entire accord with those of ultra-southern statesmen, Captain [Nathaniel] Lyon, of the United States Army, stationed at Jefferson Barracks near St. Louis, determined to strike a blow at incipient secession by the capture of General Frost and his eight hundred militiamen at Camp Jackson.[5] This was effected without resistance [on May 10, 1861], and Gen. Frost and his men were marched through the city in triumph for confinement at the United States Arsenal.[6]

The force effecting this capture was mostly German volounteers of St. Louis, hastily mustered into the service of the Government for this special service. It was a duty peculiarly agreeable, since the militia of Camp Jackson were of the higher classes, and consequently most odious to these radical foreign democrats.[7]

4. Camp Jackson, named for the governor, was about three miles west of downtown St. Louis, on the present-day campus of Saint Louis University. Frost, a New Yorker, was a member of the U.S. Military Academy's class of 1844 and was a brigadier general in the Missouri state militia. See Ezra J. Warner, *Generals in Gray: Lives of the Confederate Commanders* (Baton Rouge: Louisiana State University, 1959), 94–95.

5. Nathaniel Lyon, a Connecticut native and member of the West Point class of 1841, commanded the St. Louis arsenal in 1861. See Ezra J. Warner, *Generals in Blue: Lives of the Union Commanders* (Baton Rouge: Louisiana State University Press, 1964), 286–87; Christopher Phillips, *Damned Yankee: The Life of General Nathaniel Lyon* (Columbia: University of Missouri Press, 1990). Jefferson Barracks, about eleven miles southwest of downtown St. Louis, was the largest military post west of the Mississippi before the Civil War (William E. Parrish, "Jefferson Barracks," in Howard R. Lamar, ed., *The New Encyclopedia of the American West* [New Haven, Conn.: Yale University Press, 1998], 571).

6. The May 10 capture and subsequent events are examined in Parrish, *Turbulent Partnership*, 22–24. Lyons's larger force of ten thousand convinced Frost, with fewer than one thousand men, to surrender without resistance.

7. Walker was a member of a prominent Missouri family and obviously sympathized with the pro-southern "higher classes" at Camp Jackson. See Louis S. Gerteis, *Civil War St. Louis* (Lawrence: University Press of Kansas, 2001), 73.

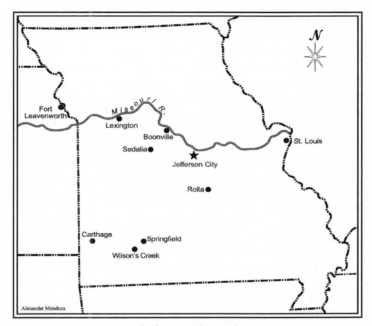

Fort
Leavenworth

M i s s o u r i R.

Lexington

Boonville

St. Louis

Sedalia

★
Jefferson City

Rolla

Carthage

Springfield

Wilson's Creek

Alexander Mendoza

Civil War Missouri

In marching their captives through the city, under the pretense that a rescue was intended, the German volunteers fired upon the people in the streets, and a number of persons were killed and wounded, a large majority of whom were women and children who had been drawn to the spot from curiosity.[8] This assault upon the sovereign state of Missouri, and followed up by almost daily outrages upon the peaceful citizens of St. Louis by the hirelings of the Federal Government, exasperated the people beyond the power of endurance, and everywhere they fled to arms.[9]

The State Convention which had met in December, and again

8. Walker accepted pro-southern accounts of the incident. A recent history of St. Louis during the war described an accidental initial shot fired by a soldier and then a general outbreak of confused firing on both sides. About twenty-eight people were killed, and dozens of others were wounded, including women and children. See Parrish, *Turbulent Partnership,* 23–24; Gerteis, *Civil War St. Louis,* 107–10.

9. Estimates vary, but about 40,000 Missouri men joined the Confederate

[in] February, had reflected the will of the people in refusing co-operation with the Southern States in seceding from the Union; but now driven to madness by the unwise aggressions of the Federal authority, and the brutality of the military chiefs at the head of which was Lyon, an enterprising but unscrupulous officer, the public sentiment of the State in May was largely in opposition to the cause of the Union. Taking advantage of this change Governor Jack[son] hastily assembled several thousand militia at Jefferson City, the capital of the state, to resist any attempted advance of Federal troops toward the interior.[10] Major General Sterling Price was appointed by the Governor[,] Commander of the State Forces, and every preparation, which the limited military resources of the state permitted, was made to resist the unwarranted and unconstitutional measures of the general government.[11]

The latter now became alarmed for the loyalty of the people of the state, which they were rapidly losing under the brutal administration of Lyon, determined upon a more conciliatory policy, and dispatched to St. Louis Brigadier General [William S.] Harney, an old officer of the army and a Southern man by birth, to relieve Captain Lyon.[12]

Although a man of limited capacity, Harney seemed to have been sincerely desirous of allaying the popular discontent, and of harmonizing Federal and State authority. As a representative of the former he concluded an arrangement with Governor Jackson by which both should henceforth be confined to their legitimate and constitutional limits; Jackson on his part stipulating

---

army, and more than 100,000 served in the Union cause. See Mark A. Lause, "Missouri," in Heidler and Heidler, *Encyclopedia of the American Civil War*, 1340.

10. Jefferson City was about 125 road miles west of St. Louis.

11. Sterling Price, a former governor of the state (1853–57), had also served as a colonel in the Mexican War. See Warner, *Generals in Gray*, 246–47; Albert Castel, *General Sterling Price and the Civil War in the West* (Baton Rouge: Louisiana State University Press, 1968).

12. Harney was not sent to St. Louis to relieve Lyon. He was commander of the army's Department of the West (with headquarters in St. Louis) when secession began and, thereby, Lyon's superior. His southern sympathies were obvious, and the army soon relieved him and placed Lyon in command in Missouri (Warner, *Generals in Blue*, 208–9; Parrish, *Turbulent Partnership*, 16–19, 25–30).

that he would disband the State forces. His part of the agreement was at once carried out, and the militia [were] disbanded and sent to their homes; and had the Federal government acted with good faith the horrors of four years of civil war in Missouri would have been avoided. Unfortunately Harney's acts were disavowed, and Harney himself recalled and Lyon, now advanced to the rank of Brigadier General, was assigned to the command in Missouri.

[The] Governor and General Price fearing that this change of commanders was a virtual disavowal and repudiation of the agreement with Gen. Harney, visited St. Louis to ascertain from his successor the sentiments and intentions of the Federal Government toward the State. They were received [on June 11] with haughty insolence by Lyon and threatened with the entire suppression of the State government unless the unconstitutional acts of the Federal government should be acquiesced in, and Missouri should furnish her contingent of troops for the coercion of her sister Southern States.[13] Jackson, warned by the expression of popular opposition to a permanent secession from the Union, was now sincerely desirous of preventing the effusion of blood, since it could not under existing conditions be productive of any useful political or military combination, or be of any service to the cause of the Confederacy which had now been formed. The humility with which Jackson listened to these insults did not, as he hoped, prevent further aggression on the part of the Federal commander. On the contrary, it emboldened him to push his policy to the utmost, and shortly after the interview General Lyon marched toward the interior with several thousand volounteers, mostly Germans and Irish. Jefferson City, the State Capital, was hastily evacuated by the State Government, and the Records removed further to the interior.[14]

13. The stormy meeting ended with this warning from Lyon: "Better, sir, far better that the blood of every man, woman, and child within the limits of the State should flow, than that she should defy the federal government. This means war." See Phillips, *Damned Yankee,* 214. Walker was clearly put off by Lyon's blustering tone.

14. Accounts of Lyon's offensive are in Phillips, *Damned Yankee,* 215–20; Robert E. Shalhope, *Sterling Price: Portrait of a Southerner* (Columbia: University of Missouri Press, 1971), 216–17.

Hearing that Governor Jackson had established the State Government at Boonville, Lyon pushed forward to that point. Here he found a few companies of raw militia, hastily assembled under the command of Colonel [John S.] Marmaduke, which he easily dispersed, as they were poorly armed with common fowling pieces, and insufficiently supplied with ammunition.[15] Here was shed the first blood in actual warfare in the contest that for four years drenched this unhappy state in blood.[16]

If the unscrupulous conduct of Lyon at St. Louis had forced the people into resistance, his activity and enterprise had ~~now~~ done much towards crushing the rebellion in Missouri. He was now in possession of the heart of the State, with a considerable military force which he could throw into the disaffected regions to crush the incipient risings of the people.[17] The possession of the Mississippi River [*he meant* Missouri River] in particular was of immense importance, enabling him to move his troops rapidly through the heart of the disaffected region, and to its western frontier, at the same time that it hopelessly separated the Governor, Jackson, from the assistance expected from the populous and thoroughly disaffected counties lying north of the Missouri river, which henceforth through the war were held to sullen and disturbed neutrality.[18] It could not, however, prevent local disturbances, or the occasional escape of bands of Southern sympathizers from crossing stealthily the [Missouri] river, and joining Governor Jackson and General Price, who now retired towards the south western corner of the state, where they hoped to receive

15. Marmaduke, a Missouri native who had studied at Yale and Harvard before graduation from the U.S. Military Academy in 1857, was a militia colonel in 1861 (Warner, *Generals in Gray*, 211–12).

16. The affair at Boonville, about 140 miles northwest of St. Louis, was barely more than a skirmish between 450 Missouri militia and Lyon's 1,700 Federals. See Phillips, *Damned Yankee*, 219–20.

17. Lyon's column grew after Boonville to 2,350 by early July. See Phillips, *Damned Yankee*, 226.

18. Several central-Missouri counties (north of the Missouri River), populated mostly by southerners and heavily pro-southern in their culture and politics, have been known as "Little Dixie" ever since the Civil War. See Robert M. Crisler, "Missouri's Little Dixie," *Missouri Historical Review* 42 (January 1948): 130–39.

assistance in men and arms from the Confederates in Arkansas, and to rally the people to the standard of the insulted and invaded State.[19]

To break up this nucleus of rebellion, a regiment of German volounteers, and a light battery under Colonel [Franz] Segel [Sigel], the same whom Stonewall Jackson afterwards so thoroughly disposed of in the Shenandoah Valley,[20] was dispatched by railway to Rolla,[21] and marching westward encountered the Missourians upon the open prairie near Carthage, where, with his usual bad fortune, he was completely defeated, and owed his escape to the unskilfulness of the inexperienced officers opposed to him, rather than to his own skill.[22]

Upon the receipt of this information Lyon with the forces under his own immediate command, moved southward from Sedalia, and forming a junction at Springfield with his discomforted subordinate and a column of regulars and Kansas volounteers from Fort Leavenworth,[23] ~~Lyon~~ found himself at the head of a well armed and equipped force of seven thousand infantry and fifteen hundred cavalry.[24] A few miles from there lay Price with his poorly armed and scarcely organized militia, now strengthened by a brigade of three thousand Confederates under Brig. Gen. [Ben] McCulloch.[25] Numerically the two armies were nearly matched, but

19. Castel, *General Sterling Price,* 26–27; Shalhope, *Sterling Price,* 167.

20. Trained in a German military academy, Sigel was a veteran of the European insurrections of 1848 who had fled to the United States in 1852 (Stephen D. Engle, *Yankee Dutchman: The Life of Franz Sigel* [Baton Rouge: Louisiana State University, 1999]). Walker referred to Sigel's rough handling by Confederate General Thomas J. (Stonewall) Jackson during the famous Valley Campaign of 1862.

21. Rolla is in central Missouri, about one hundred straight-line miles southwest of St. Louis.

22. William Garrett Piston and Richard W. Hatcher III, *Wilson's Creek: The Second Battle of the Civil War and the Men Who Fought It* (Chapel Hill: University of North Carolina Press, 2000), 103–4. Carthage is in southwest Missouri, near the Kansas border.

23. Sedalia is about 120 road miles north of Springfield. Fort Leavenworth is about 200 road miles northwest of Springfield.

24. The best scholarly treatment of the campaign puts Lyon's strength at nearly 5,500 (Piston and Hatcher, *Wilson's Creek,* 337–38).

25. Ben McCulloch, a Tennessee native who had fought in the Texas Revo-

the Missourians and even McCullough's troops (except the 3rd. La. Volunteers, a well drilled and steady regiment under Col. [Louis] Hébert, a thorough soldier,)[26] were little better than a poorly armed mob of brave men, while the Federals were thoroughly armed and equipped, and comparatively well drilled, one third of the entire army being composed of regulars.[27]

The Confederate Generals determined to assume the offensive, and attack Lyon at Springfield, and on the night of the 9th of August arrived at Oak Hill, eight miles from that place. On his part the Federal Commander had come to the same determination, and on the same night moved out of Springfield and reached the Confederate camp at daylight on the 10th where he found the Confederates still in camp, and the night having been rainy and disagreeable McCullough had withdrawn his pickets, which enabled the Federals to effect a complete surprise, and had the advantage thus gained been rigorously pressed, the Confederates must have been completely defeated and driven from the field. The latter, however, speedily recovered from their panic, and a fierce engagement followed. On their right the Federals had gained some ground, but the unfortunate Segel was completely defeated in an attempt on the Confederate right, and the death of Gen. Lyon, heading an assault upon the Confederate position, decided the victory in favor of the Confederates;[28] and had McCullough been as skilful as he was brave and have followed up the retreating army it could not have escaped utter destruction.[29]

---

lution of 1836 and in the war with Mexico, had led secessionist Texas forces in the capture of Federal property in Texas (Thomas W. Cutrer, *Ben McCulloch and the Frontier Military Tradition* [Chapel Hill: University of North Carolina Press, 1993]).

26. Louis Hébert, a Louisiana sugar planter, ranked third in his West Point class of 1845. See Warner, *Generals in Gray*, 130–31.

27. Actually, the coalition of green Missouri and Arkansas militia plus McCulloch's brigade were about twice as numerous as Lyon's force, but 20 percent of Lyon's men were soldiers in the regular U.S. Army. See Piston and Hatcher, *Wilson's Creek*, 337–38.

28. Piston and Hatcher, *Wilson's Creek*, 265–68; Phillips, *Damned Yankee*, 255–56. Oak Hill was better known as Wilson's Creek.

29. Walker may have expected too much of McCulloch and the inexperienced Confederates, who were apparently nearly as exhausted and disorganized in victory as the Federals were in defeat. See Piston and Hatcher, *Wilson's Creek*, 286.

Why it was that this blunder was so frequently committed during the war by Generals whose personal courage was beyond question will always remain a mystery.[30] In this instance it probably arose from the want of agreement existing between McCullough and Price, and a mutual feeling of jealousy, perhaps, encouraged by their respective friends. From whatever cause it arose, it was to this misunderstanding, ~~perhaps~~, more than to any other cause, that the Federal Army owed its safety. Pursuing its march without molestation to Rolla it found itself at the terminus of the Southwest Branch Railroad, whence it speedily returned to St. Louis.

McCullough, with the Confederate troops under his command, soon afterwards retired into Arkansas, and during the autumn and winter remained inactive.[31]

In the meantime Gen. Price was at the head of an irregular force of Missourians, not yet mustered into the service of the Confederate States, and whose numbers cannot be stated with any certainty, as they were held by no other bond but hatred of the Federal government and a spirit of resistance to its authority. In the early part of September [1861], however, Price moved from Springfield upon Lexington, on the Missouri river, strongly fortified and held by a garrison of thirty five hundred Irish volunteers from Chicago, Ill[.,] under the command of Col. [James A.] Mulligan. On the 17th the place was invested, and, after a short resistance, was forced to surrender on the 20th. of September.[32]

Upon the information of Price's movements reaching the Federal headquarters at St. Louis large bodies of troops were hastily pushed up the Missouri river as far as Sedalia, from which posi-

30. Walker's complaint that McCulloch and, later, other Confederate generals did not follow up on victory may have been a reflection of his own frustration during the 1864 Red River Campaign, when a defeated Federal army was allowed to retreat three hundred miles to safety in New Orleans.

31. Walker's comments on the post-battle movements of both armies were accurate. See Piston and Hatcher, *Wilson's Creek*, 305–7; Cutrer, *Ben McCulloch*, 254.

32. By the time Price reached Lexington, about 150 miles north of Springfield and 50 miles east of Kansas City, his 7,000-man army had grown with volunteers to around 10,000. Mulligan's Federal force numbered about 2,700. See Castel, *General Sterling Price*, 50–56; James A. Mulligan, "The Siege of Lexington, Mo.," in Robert Underwood Johnson and Clarence Clough Buel, eds., *Battles and Leaders of the Civil War*, 4 vols. (New York: Century, 1887–88), vol. 1: 307–13.

tion they were hurried southward to interrupt Gen. Price's retreat into Arkansas.[33]

Although Price made good his retreat it was only with a tithe of the force that assisted in the reduction of Lexington, the larger part of his army, grown tired of the war, and the hardships incident to the life of a soldier, retired to their homes.[34] The movement of Federal troops to intercept Price was set on foot by Fremont, who in October found himself in the neighborhood of Springfield, Mo.[,] at the head of a formidable force amounting to, perhaps, forty thousand effective men. Before anything was accomplished, however, Fremont was relieved of his command by Gen. [David] Hunter, who, finding it impracticable to push his column farther southward at this late season of the year, abandoned southwestern Missouri, and removed his army into winter quarters at St. Louis and the towns upon the Missouri river.[35]

33. Major General John C. Frémont led 38,000 Federals up the Missouri River to confront Price. Frémont, already famous as the "pathfinder of the West" for his explorations in the 1840s, was commander of the Department of the West, headquartered in St. Louis. See Castel, *General Sterling Price*, 57; Tom Chaffin, *Pathfinder: John Charles Frémont and the Course of American Empire* (New York: Hill and Wang, 2002).

34. Price's column dwindled from perhaps 20,000 men, mostly undisciplined civilians, after the victory at Lexington to only 7,000 nine days later (Castel, *General Sterling Price*, 57).

35. Hunter was a graduate of the West Point class of 1822. See Edward A. Miller, *Lincoln's Abolitionist General: The Biography of David Hunter* (Columbia: University of South Carolina Press, 1997).

CHAPTER 2.

Operations in the Trans-Mississippi States in 1862

In the early Spring of this year the Federal Army, twenty thousand strong, under Major General [Samuel R.] Curtis, was put in motion from St. Louis for the invasion of Arkansas via South Western Missouri.[1] Price, who during the winter had occupied that portion of the latter State, with his headquarters at Springfield, rapidly fell back into Arkansas at the approach of Curtis, until uniting again with the Confederate forces now under the command of Major General [Earl] Vandorn, who had now assumed the chief command,[2] the battle of Pea Ridge, or Elk Horn, was fought on the 5th of March, a severe but indecisive action,[3] in which Brig. Genl's McCullough and [James M.] McIntosh were killed, and the Confederate army so weakened by its losses that Gen. Van Dorn was compelled to decline a second battle and retreat.

The enemy, however, were too much crippled to follow, and in the meantime the loss of Fort Donelson and the evacuation of Kentucky, Nashville, and all of middle Tennessee by Gen. Albert Sidney Johnston decided the Government at Richmond to recall Van Dorn with the greater portion of his army to reinforce Genl. John-

1. Curtis was a member of the U.S. Military Academy class of 1831. His army, headquartered at Rolla, included about twelve thousand men. See Warner, *Generals in Blue,* 107–8; William L. Shea and Earl J. Hess, *Pea Ridge: Civil War Campaign in the West* (Chapel Hill: University of North Carolina Press, 1992), 5, 7, 14.

2. Van Dorn, a Mississippi native (West Point class of 1842), had recently been appointed commander of the new Military District of the Trans-Mississippi, thus making Price and McCulloch his subordinates. See Arthur B. Carter, *Tarnished Cavalier: Major General Earl Van Dorn* (Knoxville: University of Tennessee Press, 1999).

3. Although some Confederates, like Walker, long afterward thought of it as a tactical stalemate, the battle gave substantial control of southern Missouri to Federal forces for the rest of the war. Shea and Hess, *Pea Ridge,* esp. 259–60.

ston,[4] leaving the defence of the Confederate territory west of the Mississippi to such forces as might be organized out of the State militia of the respective states.

At this juncture Gen. Price and the greater portion of the Missouri State troops passed into the regular Confederate Service, and under Van Dorn crossed the Mississippi River and not long after the battle of Shiloh joined the army of Tennessee under Gen. [P. G. T.] Beauregard.[5]

The evacuation of New Orleans by the Confederate forces, and its occupation by the Federal forces on the 25th of April, 1862, was not so much the result of total incapacity of the Confederate General as the vicious and ruinous clashing of authority between the naval and military commanders who acted independently of each other, thus affording but little co-operative support ~~to each other~~ in the defense of the city.[6]

The possession of the defenses at the south of the Mississippi, and the capture of New Orleans opened to the Federals the heart of the South, and their gunboats and steam frigates could now ascend the river without molestation as far as Vicksburg, Miss.[,] where some hastily constructed works, upon which were mounted a few guns of heavy caliber, offered now the only obstacle to the free navigation of the enemy's vessels from the Gulf of Mexico to the Mouth of the Ohio.[7]

It will be remembered that the Confederate position of Fort Pillow, at Columbus, Kentucky, had been abandoned, and lastly, on the 5th of April, Island № 10, had, after a vigorous resistance,

4. The order to Van Dorn is in War Department, *The War of the Rebellion: A Compilation of the Official Records of the Union and Confederate Armies,* 128 vols. (Washington: Government Printing Office, 1880–1901), ser. 1, vol. 10, pt. 2: 354 (cited hereafter as *Official Records,* with all references to series 1).

5. *Official Records* 8: 813, 814; Castel, *General Sterling Price,* 82

6. For the poor coordination of land and naval defenses of New Orleans, see Charles L. Dufour, *The Night the War Was Lost* (Garden City, N.Y.: Doubleday & Co., 1960), 291–92, 339–42, 346.

7. River defenses at Port Hudson, twenty-five water miles upriver from Baton Rouge, Louisiana, were built up later in 1862 and became another serious obstacle to Federal navigation of the lower Mississippi River. See Lawrence Lee Hewitt, *Port Hudson, Confederate Bastion on the Mississippi* (Baton Rouge: Louisiana State University Press, 1987).

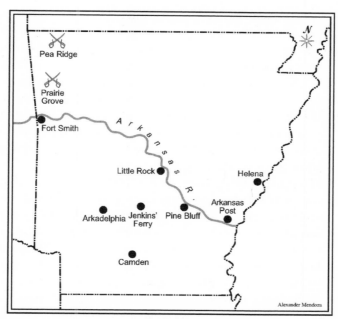

Civil War Arkansas

fallen into the enemy's hands,[8] thus sweeping away every obstacle to the free passage of the enemy's fleet as far down as Vicksburg, the possession of which became a vital necessity to the Confederates as Vicksburg was now the only remaining link connecting the Confederate States with those west of the Mississippi.[9]

The Federal forces during the summer and early autumn of 1862 made some feeble and ineffective attempts to reduce the place, principally by cutting a canal of sufficient depth to float

8. Island № 10, about forty miles downriver from Fort Pillow, was surrendered by the Confederates on April 8, 1862. They abandoned Fort Pillow in early June.

9. Walker here apparently overlooked the fact that Port Hudson, about 115 air miles and 250 river miles downstream from Vicksburg, became another Confederate strongpoint on the river a few months later. Indeed, the space between the two bastions allowed Confederates to cross men and supplies between the Trans-Mississippi theater and areas east of the river until both fell in July 1863.

gunboats & transports across a peninsular [*sic*] on the right bank of the river formed by the Mississippi river making a sharp and long detour toward the east [*actually* northeast], which after passing Vicksburg turns sharply to the westward [south-southwest]. Across the peninsular formed[,] Gen. [Benjamin F.] Butler conceived the idea of cutting a canal, by which he hoped to gain the complete control of the Mississippi.[10] The failure of this attempt, however, at the close of 1862 left the Confederates in possession of an available crossing of the Mississippi by which troops and supplies could reach the theatre of war in the East.

After the battle of Pea Ridge, or Elk Horn, as it is called by the Confederates, the Federal General Curtis, after awaiting the arrival of reinforcements and supplies from St. Louis, his real base of operations, resumed his march towards Little Rock, the capital of the State of Arkansas, via Batesville and Jacksonport on White River.[11] Van Dorn having withdrawn with all his infantry to the eastern side of the Mississippi, the defense of Arkansas devolved upon Major General [Thomas C.] Hindman,[12] who with a few regiments of Texas and Arkansas cavalry, some of which he dismounted, much to their discontent, and converted into infantry, formed [illegible word] the basis of a body of infantry which afterwards attained a high degree of efficiency and played an important part in the after history of the war west of the Mississippi.[13] Gen. Hindman was an officer of great administrative ability but not being a military man by profession was, unfortunately, ignorant of those details necessary to the successful organization

10. Although the cut became known as "Grant's Canal," the idea was originally hatched in the fertile mind of Union Major General Benjamin F. Butler. See *Official Records* 15: 25–26; Michael B. Ballard, *Vicksburg: The Campaign That Opened the Mississippi* (Chapel Hill: University of North Carolina Press, 2004), 48, 51, 55, 490.

11. Batesville and Jacksonport are about ninety-five road miles northeast of Little Rock. Curtis planned a long roundabout approach to the Arkansas capital.

12. Hindman, a veteran of the war with Mexico, had been a leading secessionist in 1861 (Warner, *Generals in Gray*, 137–38; Diane Neal and Thomas W. Kremm, *Lion of the South: General Thomas C. Hindman* [Macon, Ga.: Mercer University Press, 1993]).

13. The "body of infantry" Walker referred to so obliquely was the Texas division that he would command in the second half of the war.

of crude masses of men into formidable armies. Yet by untiring energy and by continually harrassing the enemy, cutting off their supply trains, and by the skilful use of deceptive dispatches which he contrived for the enemy to capture, so exaggerated his strength as completely to deceive Gen. Curtis and decide him to abandon the attempt on Little Rock and to reach the Mississippi [River] by the shortest route.[14] This point was Helena, a town in Arkansas some forty miles above the mouth of White River and fifty below Memphis. Here the Federal commander was safe, and here his army was broken up and transferred to such fields of operations as most required reinforcement.

In the meantime the Federal General [John M.] Schofield, in command of the district of country including Missouri and Kansas, pushed forward another army under Gen. [James G.] Blount [Blunt] into the northwestern part of the state of Arkansas with the apparent object of occupying Fort Smith at the head of navigation on the Arkansas river, and the key to the country occupied by the Indian tribes who had espoused the Confederate cause.[15]

Major General [Theophilus H.] Holmes of the Confederate army in August 1862, by orders from Richmond, had assumed command of all the Confederate forces and territory west of the Mississippi, which was afterwards officially known as the Trans-Mississippi Department.[16] To meet the threatened advances upon Fort Smith,

14. Hindman's persistent resistance was not the only reason Curtis turned away from Little Rock. Just as important was the great difficulty of supplying the Federal army away from easily navigable rivers, where Federal gunboats and supply vessels could provide a lifeline. See William L. Shea, "1862: 'A Continual Thunder,'" in Mark K. Christ, ed., *Rugged and Sublime: The Civil War in Arkansas* (Fayetteville: University of Arkansas Press, 1994), 41–42; Bobby Roberts, "Rivers of No Return," in Mark K. Christ, ed., *The Earth Reeled and Trees Trembled: Civil War Arkansas, 1863–1864* (Little Rock, Ark.: Old State House Museum, 2007), 74–89.

15. Schofield (West Point class of 1853) was then commander of the Army of the Frontier, operating in northern Arkansas. Blunt was an outspoken Kansas abolitionist. Fort Smith is about 125 straight-line miles northwest of Little Rock, on the western border of the state. See Warner, *Generals in Blue*, 37–38, 425–26; Donald B. Connelly, *John M. Schofield and the Politics of Generalship* (Chapel Hill: University of North Carolina Press, 2006).

16. Holmes, a graduate of the U.S. Military Academy in 1829, had served with distinction in the Mexican War, earning the admiration of Jefferson Davis.

General Hindman, now occupying that point, was directed to assume the offensive. He accordingly crossed Boston mountain, a spur of the Ozark range, and attacked the enemy at Prairie Grove, fifty miles north of Fort Smith, where an obstinate and bloody engagement took place on the 2nd of December which was, as was so often the case in the war, indecisive. A twenty four hours' truce was agreed upon, at the end of which time the Confederate army for the want of subsistence withdrew and took up its old position at Fort Smith, south of the Arkansas river. This closed the campaign of 1862 in Arkansas.[17]

The portion of Louisiana west of the Mississippi was in the possession of the Confederate forces except the banks of that river which was dominated by Federal gunboats. After the fall of New Orleans, Gen. [Benjamin F.] Butler, the Federal Commander, set on foot several small expeditions into the interior, principally into the rich sugar-growing region to the westward of New Orleans known as the Bayou Têche country.[18] Such resistance as was offered was by the local militia, badly armed and imperfectly organized, and was of course ineffective. Those expeditions, however, had no military importance, and were set on foot mostly for plunder, which[,] when secured[,] the expeditionary forces would return to New Orleans. One of those incursions was made in order to break up the "Salt Works," near new Iberia, which was supposed

---

After undistinguished duty in the Civil War's eastern theater, he was assigned command of the Trans-Mississippi Department in the summer of 1862, succeeding the unpopular Hindman. See Warner, *Generals in Gray,* 141; Anne J. Bailey, "Trans-Mississippi Department," in Richard N. Current, ed., *Encyclopedia of the Confederacy,* 4 vols. (New York: Simon & Schuster, 1993), vol. 4: 1607.

17. Walker's account was essentially correct except for the date of the battle (December 7). Prairie Grove resulted in the permanent Confederate loss of northwest Arkansas. See William L. Shea, *Fields of Blood: The Prairie Grove Campaign* (Chapel Hill: University of North Carolina Press, 2009).

18. Major General Butler, a Massachusetts lawyer and politician, was one of President Abraham Lincoln's "political generals," men appointed to military office primarily because of their political influence. Imaginative, slippery, and aggressive, he was commander of Federal forces in New Orleans in 1862. See Warner, *Generals in Blue,* 60–61; Hans L. Trefousse, *Ben Butler: The South Called Him Beast* (New York: Twayne Publishers, 1957).

in a great measure to supply with salt the whole of western Louisiana, Arkansas, and a portion of Texas. It seems not to have been known that these "salt works" were a stratum of unknown depth of the purest crystals, recent discovery of which had been so providential![19]

The district of Western La. was under the command of Major General [Richard] Taylor, but his small force was only sufficient to maintain a system of surveillance over the movements of the enemy, and to prevent desolation of the country by small bands of soldiers.[20] In Texas there had been no military operations during the war of sufficient importance to require notice except the surrender of the different detachments of Federal soldiery garrisoning the frontier posts at the breaking out of the war.[21] Since July 1862 the Federal naval forces had been in possession of Galveston, its principal seaport, which they acquired without bloodshed through the supineness of the Confederate commander, Brigadier General [Paul] Hébert.[22]

19. One of the largest salt deposits in North America was near New Iberia, about 140 road miles west of New Orleans (Robert L. Kerby, *Kirby Smith's Confederacy: The Trans-Mississippi South, 1863–1865* [New York: Columbia University Press, 1972], 70).

20. Taylor, son of former President Zachary Taylor and a graduate of Yale, was a Louisiana sugar planter, a former officer in Stonewall Jackson's Valley Campaign, and a naturally talented military leader. The District of West Louisiana included that part of the state west of the Mississippi River. See T. Michael Parrish, *Richard Taylor: Soldier Prince of Dixie* (Chapel Hill: University of North Carolina Press, 1992).

21. Secessionist Texans had confiscated Federal military property worth three million dollars and arranged the evacuation of two thousand Federal troops from the state in February 1861, all without violence. See Ralph Wooster, *Texas and Texans in the Civil War* (Austin, Texas: Eakin Press, 1995), 15–19.

22. The U.S. naval blockade of Galveston was tightened in the summer of 1862, but the city was not occupied until October 1862. Hébert, the Confederate commander, believed the island city was indefensible and evacuated it before Federals seized it. See Stephen R. Wise, *Lifeline of the Confederacy: Blockade Running During the Civil War* (Columbia: University of South Carolina Press, 1988), 83–86; Warner, *Generals in Gray*, 131–32; Edward T. Cotham Jr., *Battle on the Bay: The Civil War Struggle for Galveston* (Austin: University of Texas Press, 1998).

The foregoing résumé will give the reader an understanding of the military situation in the Trans-Mississippi region at the close of the year 1862. New Year's day 1863 was signalised by the recapture of Galveston by the Confederate forces under Major General [John B.] Magruder who had relieved Brigadier General Hébert in the previous August.[23] This gallant exploit illustrates what may sometimes be effected by audacity against all the suggestions of prudence and even common sense.

The city of Galveston is built on the north eastern extremity of an island of the same name, some thirty miles in length and separated from the mainland by what is known as the Western Bay, about two miles in width, which is spanned by the Houston and Galveston Railroad bridge, some five miles from the city. Lying in the harbor were three [U.S. Navy] Men of War, of which the Harriet Lane, a steam corvette of some ~~three~~ eight hundred tons, and carrying twelve heavy guns, was one.[24] This force being considered capable of holding the city against all odds, since the Confederates were thought to be unable to escape with this powerful naval force, no pickets or guards were posted at the bridge, although a regiment of Massachusetts volunteers had been landed and were quartered in a building near the piers.

The Confederate attack was made by land and water, Gen. Magruder himself leading the land forces, while the forces going by water were led by Brig. Gen. Thomas Green.[25] This consisted of two ordinary river steamers of frailest construction with the "guards"

23. Magruder (West Point class of 1830) had been cited for gallantry in the war with Mexico and had confounded the Federal army for weeks during the Peninsula Campaign in Virginia in the spring of 1862 (Warner, *Generals in Gray*, 207–8; Thomas M. Settles, *John Bankhead Magruder: A Military Reappraisal* [Baton Rouge: Louisiana State University, 2009]).

24. The *Harriet Lane*, a 750-ton side-wheeler, had been part of the U.S. naval force that captured New Orleans. See Paul H. Silverstone, *Warships of the Civil War Navies* (Annapolis, Md.: Naval Institute Press, 1989), 82.

25. Green, a Virginian by birth, had moved to Texas in 1835 and fought at the Battle of San Jacinto in the Texas Revolution. He was not promoted to the rank of brigadier general until after the Galveston fight. See Warner, *Generals in Gray*, 117–18; Odie B. Faulk, *General Tom Green, Fightin' Texan* (Waco, Texas: Texian Press, 1963).

upon the upper and lower deck strengthened by a row of cotton bales placed from stem to stern for the protection of the troops on board, which consisted of about five hundred cavalrymen armed with carbines and Enfield rifles, who volunteered for the service. Gen. Magruder succeeded in crossing the railroad bridge about 12 o'clock at night, and gained the water's edge without giving the alarm to the enemy, and after waiting some hours for the co-operation of Gen. Green, fearing that his boats had grounded in the Bay, opened fire upon the Harriett Lane, and the building in which the Mass. Infantry was quartered. The enemy's vessels returned the fire although in the darkness with such effect as to silence Gen. Magruder's guns, and he was about to withdraw to the mainland when by the light of early dawn he saw approaching Green's little steamers. Two vessels of the enemy, anchored some three quarters of a mile from the pier to which the Harriett Lane was tied, were passed in the darkness without being observed. The Confederate plan was to steer directly for the Harriett Lane when the infantry was to clear the deck by their fire, then to lay alongside and carry her by boarding. This was successfully accomplished. The Harriett Lane's fire did not stop the progress of the Confederate steamers, from whose decks was soon poured so effective a fire that the crew of the enemy's vessel were either killed or driven below, and in a few minutes her decks were in the possession of Green and his gallant men, when it was found that the Commander, Captain [Jonathan M.] Wainwright, and every commissioned officer had been killed at their posts.[26]

The Confederates[,] once in possession of the Harriett Lane[,] the expectation was that they could easily capture the smaller vessels in the harbor, but, unfortunately, one of the Confederate steamers had run her bow under the paddle wheels of the Harriett Lane with such violence as to careen her almost on her beam ends toward the land, thus making it impossible to depress her guns so as to bear upon her late friends, and it was as equally impossible for the time to get under weigh. This fact being unsuspected by the

26. Wainwright was killed by the boarding party. A few Federal officers did survive the fight. See Cotham, *Battle on the Bay,* 126, 138–39.

enemy, he blew up one of his vessels that grounded in leaving the harbor, the Federal Naval Commander perishing on board, it was supposed purposely sacrificing himself through mortification.[27]

The fruits of this gallant exploit were one war steamer, carrying sixteen guns, four hundred and sixty prisoners of war, and the recovery of the City and harbor of Galveston which was held by the Confederates to the end of the war.

In the latter part of January the Federal Commander at New Orleans Gen. [Nathaniel P.] Banks seems to have entertained the idea of invading Texas from the Gulf coast.[28] A column of some eight thousand men under Gen. [Francis J.] Herren was landed from transports west of Matagorda Bay, the entrance to which was guarded by a field work containing some eight heavy guns called Fort Esperanza. The place not being defensible against a land attack by a large force was hastily abandoned.[29] This opened Matagorda Bay to the Federals['] vessels of War and Transports. It was supposed that Lavaca was to be made a base of operations, and that San Antonio, Austin, and Houston, were the objective points of the campaign. The possession of these cities, especially the latter, which is the railroad center of the State, would have decided the fate of Texas, at least for the time being. But after some inconsiderable skirmishing between the cavalry of the two armies, the

---

27. The commander of the Federal naval expedition, William B. Renshaw, blew up his flagship, the *Westfield*, to prevent its capture. The premature explosion killed Renshaw before he could get clear. He did not sacrifice himself "through mortification," as Walker assumed. Cotham, *Battle on the Bay*, 129.

28. Major General Banks, another political general, was a former governor of Massachusetts. He had succeeded Butler as commander of the Department of the Gulf in November 1862. See James G. Hollandsworth Jr., *Pretense of Glory: The Life of General Nathaniel P. Banks* (Baton Rouge: Louisiana State University Press, 2005).

29. Walker here seems to have jumbled two different operations into one. A small U.S. naval force briefly captured the fort, seventy-five air miles northeast of Corpus Christi on the Texas coast, in October 1862 and then quickly abandoned it. A larger infantry operation, in November 1863, captured the installation and held it until June 1864. In neither case was Federal Major General Francis J. Herron involved. See Stephen A. Townsend, *The Yankee Invasion of Texas* (College Station: Texas A&M University Press, 2006), 28–31; J. Barto Arnold III, "Fort Esperanza," in Ron Tyler et al., eds., *The New Handbook of Texas*, 6 vols. (Austin: Texas State Historical Assn., 1996): vol. 2: 1100.

Federal troops re-embarked and returned to New Orleans. From this time to the end of the war, Texas was freed from the presence of the enemy except a small garrison principally of negro troops at Point Isabel at the mouth of the Rio Grande.[30]

Galveston and Matamoras [across the Rio Grande from Brownsville, Texas] became the center of a flourishing trade in contraband goods in exchange for cotton, and through these ports the Confederate armies west of the Mississippi were supplied with arms, munitions of war and clothing, but less thoroughly than they might have been under a commander of more military ability than Gen. E. Kirby Smith, and under a better system than the vicious bureaucracy instituted by the Central Government at Richmond.[31] In the management of cotton there was much ground of complaint both from the planter whose property was impressed by agents of the Government, and paid for at a nominal price in Confederate currency, and from the army, which, notwithstanding the vast amount of cotton passing continually to market, was always in a chronic state of destitution of shoes, blankets, and woolen clothing.[32]

One of these agents [of the Confederate government], holding the nominal rank of major in the army, furnished, so far as it is known, the sole example, on the Confederate side, of treasonable correspondence with the enemy on the ~~point~~ part of a commissioned officer, during the entire war.

30. Walker was apparently not aware of how extensive Banks's operations along the lower coast and up the Rio Grande were in 1863–64. For a history of those operations, see Townsend, *Yankee Invasion of Texas*; Wooster, *Texas and Texans in the Civil War*.

31. Edmund Kirby Smith, a member of the West Point class of 1845, had fought with distinction in the war with Mexico and on the Indian frontier. He had led one of the Confederate armies in the 1862 Kentucky Campaign. Appointed to command the Trans-Mississippi Department in late 1862, he earned only minimal admiration from Walker, who believed Smith was out of his depth. See Warner, *Generals in Gray*, 279–80.

32. See James W. Daddysman, *The Matamoros Trade: Confederate Commerce, Diplomacy, and Intrigue* (Newark: University of Delaware Press, 1984); Kerby, *Kirby Smith's Confederacy*, 155–207; Judith F. Gentry, "White Gold: The Confederate Government and Cotton in Louisiana," *Louisiana History* 33 (Spring 1992): 229–40.

The correspondence of Major [Andrew W.] Mc.Kee, the person alluded to, with the enemy was intercepted and shown to contain the exact information of the strength and position of the Confederate forces. He was tried by court martial, convicted, and ordered to be executed, but escaped through the intervention of the civil courts and a writ of <u>habeas corpus</u>.[33]

The commencement of military operations in Arkansas in 1863 was most unfortunate for the Confederate arms. A fortified position on the Arkansas river, known as the Post of the Arkansas, about forty miles from its entrance into the Mississippi, garrisoned by two brigades of Texas infantry, about thirty eight hundred strong, under Brigadier General [Thomas J.] Churchill, after sustaining a combined attack by water and land against a force of some twenty thousand infantry and a flotilla of gunboats, under the command of Gen. [John A.] McClernand, was forced to capitulate on the 14th. of January.[34]

The division of Major General John G. Walker on the first information of the advance of the enemy moved from Pine Bluff by force[d] marches to reinforce Gen. Churchill but was unable to effect a junction with the latter's forces before he had capitulated.[35] The enemy, satisfied with the fruits of their victory, immediately reembarked, and proceeded out of the river and up the Mississippi. This was the force of Gen. [William T.] Sherman returning from

33. Andrew W. McKee, the Confederate major, and his cousin J. H. McKee, on Banks's staff, apparently were fully as guilty as Walker alleged. Walker was particularly irritated by this case because he was the official forced to release the convicted McKee, who jumped bail and disappeared. See Kerby, *Kirby Smith's Confederacy*, 274–75.

34. Arkansas Post (or Fort Hindman), a threat to navigation on the Mississippi River, was seized by 37,000 Federals in combined army and naval units on January 11, 1863. Churchill's badly outnumbered Confederates (about 5,000 men) surrendered after a naval bombardment and infantry assault. See Thomas A. DeBlack, "1863: 'We Must Stand or Fall Alone,'" in Christ, ed., *Rugged and Sublime*, 59–65. For McClernand and Churchill, see Warner, *Generals in Blue*, 293–94; Warner, *Generals in Gray*, 49–50.

35. Walker referred to himself in the third person here. He had assumed command on January 1 of the Texas infantry division that would come to be identified with him. See Richard Lowe, *Walker's Texas Division, C.S.A.: Greyhounds of the Trans-Mississippi* (Baton Rouge: Louisiana State University Press, 2004), 61–64.

an unsuccessful attack upon Vicksburg, and this detour seems to have been made to cover up the disappointment of his failure there.[36]

About the middle of January Gen. Hindman, finding it impracticable to subsist his division in the exhausted country about Fort Smith, abandoned his winter quarters, and, after intense suffering from cold and hunger, his men marching upon frozen ground covered with snow, many of them without shoes, or blankets, arrived early in February at Little Rock in a deplorable condition. Men fighting for a principle, however, are not easily discouraged, and by the middle of April Hindman's division had recovered[,] by the return of stragglers to their colors, and the accession of volunteers and conscripts[,] its former strength.

Owing to a disagreement between Gen. Hindman and Gen. Holmes, the Commander of the Department, about this time the former was relieved in the command of his division and ordered east of the Mississippi, his command being assigned to Major General Sterling Price.

At this time the forces in the Trans-Mississippi Department, amounted to about fifteen thousand five hundred infantry, and six thousand cavalry, as follows: in Arkansas Major Gen. Price's Infantry, six thousand strong, Major Gen. John G. Walker's infantry division, five thousand strong, Brig. Gen. J[ohn]. S. Marmaduke's cavalry, twenty five hundred.[37] In the district of West La. the force under Major Gen. Taylor did not exceed twenty five hundred infantry, under Brig. Gen. [Alfred] Mouton, and a brigade of cavalry under Brig. Gen. Tom Green.[38]

36. This was wishful thinking by Walker. It was true that Major General Sherman had been repulsed at Chickasaw Bluffs near Vicksburg in late December, but Sherman did not command the Arkansas Post expedition. McClernand's military purpose was to remove a threat to Federal navigation of the Mississippi River.

37. The regiments in Walker's division, 12,000 strong when first formed a year earlier, had dwindled in size due to disease, deaths, desertions, resignations, reassignments, the release of some men because of age, and various other causes. Most Civil War units shook down from their original sizes in their first year.

38. Mouton, son of former governor and U.S. senator Alexander Mouton of Louisiana, was an 1850 graduate of the U.S. Military Academy. He would com-

The force under Gen. Magruder in Texas did not exceed two thousand infantry at Galveston, with three or four regiments of cavalry upon the Rio Grande and northern frontiers of the State.[39] The latter were little to be depended upon for regular warfare, since they could with difficulty be induced to go beyond the immediate neighborhood of their homes, for fear that in their absence their families might be murdered by the wild Indians who are constantly depredating upon the frontier settlements, and now more than ever, being instigated by the agents of the Federal Government, as has been officially avowed since the termination of the war.

It will be seen how inadequate such a force was for the defence of a country with an area (without including the State of Missouri) greater than France, Belgium, and Great Britain together, against a powerful enemy whose command of the sea and navigable rivers gave him the selection of the point of attack. It naturally resulted that the Federal invading columns were always successful <u>near the water,</u> and it was only when their armies attempted to penetrate to the interior, and experienced some of the same difficulties that Confederate armies had constantly to surmount, such as procuring subsistence and forage in an almost exhausted country, drawing supplies from distant bases of operations over execrable roads, and through a hostile population, that the Confederates had any chance of success.

It was, therefore, manifestly the true policy of the Confederates to decline battle upon the borders of navigable rivers and near the shores of the Gulf of Mexico; but it was urged with much justice on the other hand, that the most productive and populous portion of the Trans-Mississippi regions lie contiguous to navigable streams and near the sea coast, and to permit the enemy to possess themselves of these districts would be the loss of the means of subsis-

---

mand a brigade and eventually a division under Richard Taylor in the District of West Louisiana in 1863 and 1864. See William Arceneaux, *Acadian General Alfred Mouton and the Civil War,* 2nd ed. (Lafayette: Center for Louisiana Studies, 1981).

39. For Confederate activities on the western frontier, see David Paul Smith, *Frontier Defense in the Civil War: Texas' Rangers and Rebels* (College Station: Texas A&M University Press, 1992).

tence of our own armies without having deprived the enemy of his powers of invasion always open to him by means of his inexhaustible supplies at the North, and his unlimited means of transportation.

Such was the condition of affairs in March 1863 when Brig. Gen. Holmes was relieved of the command of the department by Lieut. Gen. E. Kirby Smith, who established his Head Quarters at Shreveport, La., a town of some ten thousand inhabitants, situated upon Red River, about two hundred and fifty miles from its junction with the Mississippi.[40]

Under the administration of Gen. Hindman during the previous Spring and Summer, and fully continued under Gen. Holmes, many workshops and manufacturies of arms, munitions of war, chemicals and clothing were set on foot in different portions of the Trans-Mississippi Valley. Gen. Smith had the good sense to appreciate the value of these works and took measures to carry them out on a scale of greater magnitude than was possible to Gen. Hindman. Ample means of effecting such desirable results as the completion of these works would ensure, were placed in the hands of Gen. Smith by the Government at Richmond by giving him complete control of the cotton belt of the country. In fact the most ample powers were conferred upon the new commander, who was known to possess in an eminent degree the confidence of President [Jefferson] Davis. In fact his Headquarters became in some measure a Ministry of War for the Trans-Mississippi Department, but without the legal authority necessary to make it effective.

The distance of this theatre of war from the seat of the central government & the exceptional condition of the Confederate armies beyond the Mississippi, would seem to have afforded an irristible [irresistible] argument against the system of Central or Aulic Councils which in all countries at some period of their histories furnished just grounds of complaint to commanders of armies in

40. Shreveport is in the northwest corner of Louisiana. Good studies of Smith and his administration include Joseph Howard Parks, *General Edmund Kirby Smith, C.S.A.* (Baton Rouge: Louisiana State University Press, 1954); Kerby, *Kirby Smith's Confederacy*; Jeffery S. Prushankin, *A Crisis in Confederate Command: Edmund Kirby Smith, Richard Taylor, and the Army of the Trans-Mississippi* (Baton Rouge: Louisiana State University Press, 2005).

Civil War Louisiana

the field.[41] It might have been hoped that a government founded in the latter half of the nineteenth century would have avoided some of the rocks so well charted by historians. But the vice of centralism seems inherent and inseparable from government whether absolute, directorial, or republican. It is to this repugnance to part with the smallest fraction of perogative [sic] and power on the part of the Richmond Government must be attributed the failure of a measure often proposed by the Confederate Congress to establish a separate Ministry of War for the Trans-Mississippi Department. In more able hands than those of Gen. Smith such a Ministry would have developed the strength and resources of the country and by the assistance it could have rendered the armies east might have changed the whole aspect of the war and perhaps its final result.

The Federal Government, although its armies had twice been

41. Here Walker complained about the reluctance of officials in the Confederate capital at Richmond, Virginia, to allow the Trans-Mississippi Department to develop and carry out its own approach to the war. "Aulic Council" refers to an office of the old Holy Roman Empire and connotes centralized control.

repulsed at Vicksburg, had not given up the idea of its capture, and early in March Gen. [Ulysses S.] Grant was placed in command of the force for its reduction.[42] His first [*sic*] attempt was a continuation of the abortive one of Gen. Butler of the year before,[43] and for several weeks thousands of laborers were employed to deepen the canal across the peninsular already referred to. Dredging boats of the most ingenious contrivance were employed to assist these labors, but to no effect.[44] The idea was then conceived by the Federal General and his engineers of actually turning the Mississippi from its bed through Lake Providence [on the Louisiana side of the river] into the Tensas River which issues from it and one hundred and twenty miles further south forms a junction with the Ouachita, a tributary of Red River.

Immense labor was expended on this wild scheme but the river was too fondly wedded to its bed to be turned aside. A steamer of moderate dimension was, however, gotten through the canal, and some distance into the Tensas River and there abandoned. This is worthy of mention as it involves a question of practical engineering much discussed.[45]

The failure to get below Vicksburg with his transports turned the attention of Gen. Grant to the plan successfully adopted by him of passing his army and the necessary supplies across the peninsular to a point below Vicksburg where he would be in communication with, and receive the assistance of, the Federal fleet which had succeeded in passing the Confederate batteries at Port Hudson, forty miles from the mouth [of the Red River], after some loss,

42. Grant had assumed command of the various offensives against Vicksburg several months earlier, in late 1862.

43. Actually, Grant's first attempt to get an army near Vicksburg had begun in the late fall of 1862 and ended with the Confederate cavalry raid at Holly Springs, Mississippi, in December 1862, forcing the Federals to retreat.

44. Grant finally abandoned the canal project in March 1863. See Ballard, *Vicksburg,* 157–59, 172.

45. Lake Providence is about forty air miles northwest of Vicksburg. The attempt to re-route the river two hundred miles through the lake and bayous and down to the Red River, like so many other plans, proved impractical, and Grant abandoned it too in late March. See Ballard, *Vicksburg,* 173–74; Edwin Cole Bearss, *The Campaign for Vicksburg,* 3 vols. (Dayton, Ohio: Morningside House, 1985–86), vol. 1: 467–78.

particularly the burning by red hot shot of the steam frigate Mississippi.[46]

It was now the season of high water, and the Mississippi, although not reaching its maximum, had overflowed most of the country over which this road [along the west bank of the Mississippi River] was to be constructed, but the Federal army, with its characteristic industry, very soon threw up an embankment of sufficient height to permit Grant's army with its immense train to pass dry shod from Milican's [Milliken's] Bend to New Carthage and thus turn the Confederate stronghold.[47]

If the overflow of the country was a serious obstacle to the accomplishment of this, on the other hand it secured Grant against interference from the Confederate troops on the western side of the river, as the country was more or less under water for fifteen miles to the westward. In order to render this non-interference with Grant's operations on the part of the Confederates more certain Gen. Banks made about the same time a movement from Berwick's Bay [in south Louisiana] through the Bayou Têche country. Major Gen. Taylor, with the forces I have already mentioned, had taken up a position a short distance from Breshear [Brashear] City, the terminus of the Opelousas and New Orleans railroad, and thrown up some field works upon both banks of the Bayou [Teche] to check the advance of the enemy.[48]

The peculiarity of the Bayou country was remarkably favorable to neutralize the great numerical superiority of the enemy. For a half mile on either side of the Bayou the land is elevated and in cultivation, principally in sugar cane, but falls off gradually into

46. A Federal fleet attempted to steam upriver to join Grant in March but was stopped by the Confederate guns at Port Hudson, where the U.S.S. *Mississippi* was burned. Grant instead relied on a different fleet from upriver to run past the batteries of Vicksburg and join him south of there. See Bearss, *Campaign for Vicksburg* 1: 679–84; Ballard, *Vicksburg,* 198–202.

47. Milliken's Bend, on the Louisiana side of the river, was upstream, 25 river miles (16 air miles) northwest of Vicksburg. New Carthage was downstream, 30 river miles (18 air miles) southwest of Vicksburg.

48. Berwick Bay, Brashear City (present-day Morgan City), and the Teche country are about ninety road miles southwest and west of New Orleans. Banks moved north, toward central Louisiana.

marshes, or swamps, as they are called, which are entirely impassable even for infantry. Of course in selecting a defensive position, reference will be had to the distance from the Bayou to the swamp. Camp Bisland seems to have been well selected since with this handful of men Gen. Taylor was enabled for more than a week to check Gen. Banks' advance.[49] He was forced at length to abandon his position, the Federal General [Cuvier] Grover having been dispatched at the head of eight thousand men on transports up Grand Lake which lies to the northward parralel [*sic*] to Bayou Têche and but a few miles distant, for the purpose of landing at the head of the lake, crossing over to Bayou Têche in the rear of Gen. Taylor and thus cutting off his retreat which could only be effected by following the road immediately upon the banks of the Bayou. This movement would have been completely successful but for the timidity and tardiness of Grover.[50] As it was[,] Taylor barely escaped by the most desperate fighting at the town of Franklin where the heads of the two columns met, Taylor retreating, Grover advancing.[51]

The desperate situation of the Confederates was apparent to the men in the ranks, and inspired them to such energy that nothing could resist the impetuosity of their onset, and the Federal army, nearly four times their strength, was driven back and the only road to the Confederate retreat secured.[52]

In the meantime Gen. Banks with the main body of his army took possession of the abandoned position at Camp Bisland and followed in the direction taken by the Confederate force. At Franklin he formed a junction with Gen. Grover and learned from him

49. Camp Bisland was a collection of low earthworks on the west bank of Bayou Teche, about twelve miles upstream from Brashear City.

50. Grover, a New Englander and a member of the West Point class of 1850, led a division of Banks's army at the engagement near Fort Bisland. See Warner, *Generals in Blue*, 193–94; Mark Mayo Boatner III, *The Civil War Dictionary*, rev. ed. (New York: David McKay Co., 1988), 426–27.

51. Franklin was several miles upstream from Camp Bisland and about twenty-two road miles northwest of Brashear City.

52. Walker's account was essentially correct. Taylor's army of about four thousand faced sixteen thousand Federals on the road from Camp Bisland to Franklin. See Kerby, *Kirby Smith's Confederacy*, 97–99.

the escape of Taylor's little army, and with his whole force, some eighteen thousand strong, took up the pursuit. It was ineffectual, however, and except the daily and almost hourly skirmishing of the Confederate rear guard, commanded by the gallant Gen. [Tom] Green of Texas, and the advance of the Federals, the march to Alexandria was unopposed. At this point he abandoned the pursuit of Gen. Taylor, turned toward the Mississippi, crossed the Atchafalya [Atchafalaya River] at Simmesport by means of the Federal fleet,[53] and embarked his army at the mouth of Red River upon steam boats, escorted by iron clads, and proceeded to invest Port Hudson, on a fortified position on the left bank of the Mississippi, eighteen miles above Baton Rouge, La. The garrison consisting of about seven thousand men, under Gen. [Franklin] Gardner, resisted all attacks, and only surrendered upon learning of the fall of Vicksburg and the failure of subsistence and ammunition.[54]

As soon as it became apparent that Gen. Banks' movements were directed to the invasion of the Opelousas and Têche districts the Confederate Gen., Taylor, made urgent demands for reinforcements, which were finally acted upon by Gen. Smith, and several regiments of newly organized mounted volunteers were ordered from Texas, and Major General Walker's division of infantry from Arkansas. The distance, however, was so great, and the condition of the roads so wretched, that the greater portion of Western La. [i.e., the region between New Orleans and Alexandria] was overrun by the enemy before these reinforcements could reach the theatre of operations.

It must be constantly borne in mind that in the Trans-Mississippi States there were no railroads except in South Eastern Texas,[55] and no navigable rivers available to the Confederate

53. The Atchafalaya begins where the Red River empties into the Mississippi and is a distributary of both the Red and Mississippi rivers. It flows south 170 miles and empties eventually into the Gulf of Mexico. Simmesport, on the west bank, is at the head of the Atchafalaya.

54. Gardner, a classmate of U. S. Grant at West Point, commanded about 6,800 Confederate defenders at Port Hudson and held off Banks's 30,000-plus army for several weeks, surrendering only after the fall of Vicksburg made Port Hudson's fate obvious. See Hewitt, *Port Hudson.*

55. It is not clear why Walker wrote that there were no railroads except in southeastern Texas. In fact, several short lines operated in the Trans-Missis-

armies except Red River, and, during a short period of the year, the Arkansas and the Ouachita.[56] To illustrate the difficulties of marching troops over the roads of that country at this season of the year, when the winter frost and snow and the rain of the early Spring had thoroughly saturated the soil, it is mentioned that Genl Walker's division was from the 25th. of April to the 7th. of May [1863] marching from Pine Bluff, Arkansas, to Monroe, La. a distance of one hundred and fifty miles.[57] Sections of roads for miles would have to be laid down, or "corduroyed," with logs to permit the passage of the baggage and subsistence trains, and bridges, carried away by the floods, reconstructed by engineer and pioneer corps.

At the period of the arrival of this division at Monroe, Gen. Grant was fighting at Baker's Creek, and Champion's Hill, and occupying Jackson, Miss.[58] He had not invested Vicksburg, the Yazoo River was still closed to him, and therefore he was forced to draw his supplies by the identical route along which he had marched his army, since Port Hudson still barred the lower Mississippi to the passage of all descriptions of vessels except the least vulnerable iron clads.[59] Consequently if Gen. [E. Kirby] Smith had thrown his

---

sippi Department: in northeastern Texas, southeastern Louisiana, northeastern Louisiana, and eastern Arkansas. In fact, Walker's own division had used the Vicksburg, Shreveport & Texas in 1863. His complex sentence structure may mean that these lines were not usually "available to the Confederate armies." See Robert C. Black, *The Railroads of the Confederacy* (Chapel Hill: University of North Carolina, 1952).

56. Smaller streams as well as some parts of the Ouachita, the Arkansas, and even the Red River were occasionally too shallow to permit regular riverboat traffic in the 1860s. Historians, archaeologists, and geographers in Arkansas and Louisiana agree with Walker on this point (e-mail messages to the editor, November 17–19, 2008, in possession of the editor, Denton, Texas).

57. Walker's division normally covered similar distances in much less time. Pine Bluff is in central Arkansas, about forty-five miles southeast of Little Rock. Monroe, eighty miles west of Vicksburg, is in northeastern Louisiana.

58. Champion Hill and Baker's Creek were east of the Mississippi River, near Jackson.

59. The Yazoo River, a few miles north of Vicksburg, would later become Grant's supply line on the east side of the Mississippi River. Until then, as Walker wrote, Grant was forced to draw supplies over the vulnerable sixty-mile-long land route along the west bank of the river. Contrary to widespread belief, then

whole force at this period upon Grant's communications from Millican's Bend to New Carthage, it would, undoubtedly, have forced the Federal General to open up his communications with the upper Mississippi at the expense of suspending operations against Vicksburg; thus giving time and opportunity of either reinforcing this important stronghold, or of permitting to Gen. [Joseph E.] Johnston the enforcement of his orders to [John C.] Pemberton to withdraw his troops.[60] The disobedience of the latter caused the Confederate cause thirty five thousand men, and was one of the principal links in the chain of misfortune by which the Confederacy was dragged down to failure and ruin.[61]

General Banks, after a brief occupation of the Red River valley, had, about the 15th of May, abandoned his conquest and marched toward Port Hudson, as has been already mentioned. The excellent division of Gen. Walker, as suggested by that General, might have rendered important service to the Confederate cause by operating against Grant's communications, but the fear entertained by Gen. Smith that Banks had ulterior designs against Shreveport and North Eastern Texas, frightened him into a refusal to permit these troops to be so employed,[62] and they were pushed forward [from Monroe] by force[d] marches, first through Shreveport to cover that place, and afterwards, when it was known to Gen. Smith that Banks had not advanced beyond Alexandria, to Natchitoches, on

---

and since, Grant did not abandon this long supply line when his army crossed to the east side of the river. See Bearss, *Campaign for Vicksburg* 2: 480–81.

60. The highest-ranking Confederate general in Mississippi, Johnston, ordered the commander of forces in Vicksburg, John C. Pemberton, to abandon the city and unite with Johnston's own army near Jackson to confront Grant together. Pemberton believed it was his duty to protect the city at all costs, and he therefore stayed in the defensive works near Vicksburg, to Walker's chagrin. See Ballard, *Vicksburg,* 282–85; Craig L. Symonds, *Joseph E. Johnston: A Civil War Biography* (New York: W. W. Norton & Co., 1992), 205–10.

61. Walker's estimate was very close. Confederate losses included 9,091 casualties (killed, wounded, and missing) during the actual campaign and 29,491 prisoners of war. See Ballard, *Vicksburg,* 398–99.

62. Walker complained about this lost opportunity to strike at Grant's vulnerable supply line on the Louisiana side of the river at the time and in his postwar memoir.

Red River, where it formed a junction with the handful of Gen. Taylor's forces which the long retreat before Banks, and the consequent demoralization, had left him.[63]

Before this time, however, the Federal General [Banks] had taken up his march for the Mississippi, but in the hope of falling upon his rear guard, at least, Walker's division was hastily embarked upon steamers and landed at Alexandria. A brigade, under Brigadier General [James M.] Hawes, was pushed forward in pursuit, but unsuccessfully,[64] as Banks' rear guard was found to have safely crossed the Atchafalaya, by means of Admiral [David D.] Porter's fleet.[65]

The Commander of the Trans-Mississippi Department now found himself in a condition of cruel isolation. With a daily increasing army, which, even now, if it could have been thrown into the contest at the vital points might have given a new character to the war in the West, and perhaps have decided the struggle in favor of Southern independence, he saw himself unable to render the least assistance, either to beleaguered Vicksburg, or Port Hudson, the guns from which could be heard without interruption. The golden opportunity had been allowed to pass, Grant had completed the investment of Vicksburg, brushed away the obstructions to the navigation of the Yazoo River by his supply vessels, and thus rendered his line of operations and supply secure from

63. Before it reached Shreveport, Walker's division was diverted farther south to Natchitoches, about sixty-five air miles southeast of Shreveport. See Lowe, *Walker's Texas Division,* 76–78.

64. Walker mistakenly referred to James M. Hawes as the commander of the pursuing Confederates. Instead, Colonel Horace Randal's brigade led the search (Lowe, *Walker's Texas Division,* 78); M. Jane Johansson, *Peculiar Honor: A History of the 28th Texas Cavalry, 1862–1865* (Fayetteville: University of Arkansas Press, 1998), 51.

65. Porter was one of the most important Federal naval officers on the Mississippi River in 1863. He had commanded the fleet that ran past Vicksburg's batteries as part of Grant's offensive. Aggressive, bombastic, and effective, he dominated naval affairs on the Mississippi between Vicksburg and the Red River. See Jack J. Cardoso, "Porter, David Dixon," in Heidler and Heidler, *Encyclopedia of the American Civil War,* 1552–54; Chester G. Hearn, *Admiral David Dixon Porter* (Annapolis, Md.: Naval Institute Press, 1996).

attack, since it was along the highway of the Mississippi and Yazoo Rivers, guarded and commanded by Federal fleets;[66] thus rendering the crossing of the Mississippi by any considerable body of Confederate troops impossible.

The imminence of the loss of Vicksburg, however, decided General Smith to attempt something for its relief, and Gen. Taylor was directed to embark his available infantry forces, with such irregular cavalry as he could collect in the district of country in Northeastern Louisiana, and proceed to a point as nearly opposite Vicksburg as practicable.

On the 31st of May these troops [Walker's Texans] reached the vicinity of Vicksburg, broke up some small encampments of Federal troops at Perkins' Landing, below Vicksburg,[67] and marched upon Millikens Bend, held by a brigade of negro troops and two regiments of Illinois volunteers. Here a fierce engagement took place between [Henry] McCullough's brigade and the Federal garrison, posted advantageously behind the levee.[68]

The impetuosity of McCullough's Texans, however, could not be resisted, and the levee was carried and almost the entire negro force was either killed, captured, or driven into the Mississippi River and drowned.[69]

66. The new supply line, from the Yazoo River to Vicksburg, began operations on May 21 while Walker's division was on the Red River, 170 road miles to the southwest. The general realized that the "golden opportunity" to strike Grant's communications has passed. See Bearss, *Campaign for Vicksburg* 3: 791–92.

67. At Perkins' Landing (twenty-five miles southwest of Vicksburg), halfway through the war, men of the Texas division experienced hostile fire for the first time. See Lowe, *Walker's Texas Division,* 82–85.

68. Milliken's Bend, a Federal strongpoint on the west bank of the Mississippi River, was twenty-five river miles upstream from Vicksburg. Until Grant opened his supply line on the east side of the river, Milliken's Bend had been a supply depot and the head of his communications on the Louisiana side of the river. By the time Walker's Texans attacked on June 7, however, the little settlement was only a recruiting center for African American troops. Henry McCulloch was the brother of Ben McCulloch, the commander of Texas troops at Wilson's Creek.

69. The assault by McCulloch's brigade pushed Federal defenders off the levee and back to the river bank. The timely arrival of Federal gunboats, which threw heavy shells among the attackers, halted the Texans' advance. See Lowe, *Walker's Texas Division,* 88–99; Noah Andre Trudeau, *Like Men of War: Black Troops in the Civil War, 1862–1865* (Boston: Little, Brown and Co., 1998), 46–59; Richard

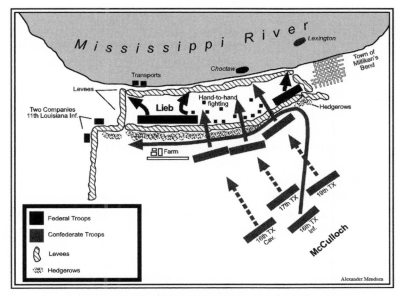

Battle of Milliken's Bend, June 7, 1863

The report of Gen. Halleck of that year puts down the Federal loss at seven hundred and eighty, not including the negro soldiers and their white officers.[70] This was the first instance during the war in which negroes in the service of the Federal government came into collision with the troops of the Confederacy, and the obstinacy with which they fought, and the loss of a hundred and twenty killed and wounded of McCullough's men, opened the eyes of the Confederates to the consequences to be apprehended by the Federal employment of these auxiliaries.[71]

Lowe, "Battle on the Levee: The Fight at Milliken's Bend," in John David Smith, ed., *Black Soldiers in Blue: African American Troops in the Civil War Era* (Chapel Hill: University of North Carolina Press, 2002), 107–35.

70. Losses at Milliken's Bend included 652 Federals (of 1,328 engaged) and 185 Confederates (of 1,500 engaged). See Lowe, "Battle on the Levee," 124.

71. Among Confederates, Walker was unusually perceptive in his early recognition of the potential value of black troops to the Union cause. He could not have known at the time that African American regiments had fought in a pitched battle for the first time only eleven days earlier at the siege of Port Hudson. See

During the action two gun boats came to the assistance of the Federal infantry, and Gen. McCullough, having now entirely dispersed and driven the negro troops into the river, very properly retired beyond the range of the enemy's guns.[72] Major General Taylor, who up to this time had directed the operation of the Confederate forces, now returned to Alexandria, leaving Major Genl. Walker in command.

The fate of Vicksburg, now besieged by at least seventy thousand infantry under Grant, and a fleet of gun boats operating above and below the city, could not be averted, or any material assistance rendered by the small force west of the Mississippi under Genl. Walker. It will be remembered that in the operations of Gen. Butler in the previous year a canal had been excavated for the purpose of opening a passage to the upper Mississippi for vessels of war and transports without the risk of passing under the fire of the Confederate batteries at Vicksburg. The attempt had not been successful, but the excavation made now afforded the besiegers excellent cover against any attempt to relieve the beleaguered city by the Confederate forces west of the Mississippi.

Gen. Taylor, upon his arrival in Alexandria, set on foot an expedition to capture the Posts in Berwick's Bay, on the Gulf of Mexico, held by the Federal forces in which he was entirely successful. Brashear City was captured, and some thirteen hundred prisoners of war and an immense booty fell into the hands of the Confederates, almost without loss on their part.[73] This is the western

---

Lawrence Lee Hewitt, "An Ironic Route to Glory: Louisiana's Native Guards at Port Hudson," in Smith, ed., *Black Soldiers in Blue*, 78–106.

72. The heavy naval guns of the U.S.S. *Choctaw*, a 1,000-ton ironclad, and the *Lexington*, a 360-ton timberclad, scattered the Texans and ended the engagement. This naval fire against exposed infantry must have reminded Walker of Malvern Hill in 1862. See Trudeau, *Like Men of War*, 57; Lowe, "Battle on the Levee," 123–24; Silverstone, *Warships of the Civil War Navies*, 157, 159.

73. Taylor captured 1,700 prisoners, thousands of small arms, hundreds of wagons, dozens of pieces of heavy and field artillery, and tons of ordnance and other supplies, enough to support his army during the 1864 Red River Campaign. See Stephen S. Michot, "In Relief of Port Hudson: Richard Taylor's 1863 Lafourche Offensive," *Military History of the West* 23 (Fall 1993): 103–34; Parrish, *Richard Taylor*, 295–305; Kerby, *Kirby Smith's Confederacy*, 118; *Official Records* 26, pt. 1: 211–12.

terminus of the Opelousas and New Orleans Railroad, and distant eighty miles from the latter, and its possession opened the road to a point opposite the city; and had the means of crossing the river been at hand the city of New Orleans, from which Gen. Banks had withdrawn all his effective forces to prosecute the siege of Port Hudson, would, doubtless, have fallen into the hands of the Confederates. As it was, after an unsuccessful attempt to capture Fort Butler at Donelsonville [Donaldsonville] on the west bank of the Mississippi,[74] in which the Confederates sustained a heavy loss, Gen. Taylor withdrew his troops beyond the Atchafalaya [River], and took up a position at Vermillionville [present-day Lafayette], with his pickets in front of Brashear City, now reoccupied by the Federal troops.

On the fourth of July the silence of the guns, whose thunder for more than seven weeks had been borne upon the eastern breeze, warned Gen. Walker that Vicksburg, the last stronghold of the Confederates on the Mississippi, had fallen into the hands of the enemy.[75] Upon ~~this~~ the confirmation of this, his division reduced from five thousand to fifteen hundred effective troops by a two months campaign in land always malarious, but rendered doubly so from the recent general overflow of the country by the Mississippi, Gen. Walker prepared to move his sick.[76] The summer fevers of this region are, fortunately, not of a dangerous type and yield readily to quinine; and in connection with the movement of the sick of this division one circumstance is worth mention.

Upon the high lands near Monroe, La. the nearest pine lands to the theatre of operations, Gen. Walker had formed a sick camp, or open air hospital, and now that his division was ordered to the valley of Red River, some one hundred miles distant, it became a serious question what was to be done with the one thousand sick men under medical treatment, and too weak, of course, to march with their commands. It was determined to move the whole number by easy marches to Nachitoches [Natchitoches] on Red River. For

74. Michot, "In Relief of Port Hudson," 120–22.

75. Walker again overlooked Port Hudson, which surrendered to Banks's Federals five days after Vicksburg fell to Grant.

76. For Walker's June–July campaign in the swamps west of the Mississippi, see Lowe, *Walker's Texas Division,* 104–6.

this purpose only twenty wagons and twelve ambulances could be procured. The Chief Surgeon, [Elias James] Beall, however, by the most judicious use of these, succeeded in moving this camp and all its sick over one hundred miles in sixteen days.[77] The plan adopted was to take the worst cases early in the morning by ambulances and wagons, and transport them say, five, six, or at most seven miles, to the encampment for the next night. The ambulances, etc, then returned for the next worst class of cases, whilst the stronger ones and the convalescents would take their own time, resting frequently under the shade of the forest through which they were passing, and reaching camp before dark. The improvement ~~of the sick~~ in the condition of the sick from the first day was marked, and upon their arrival at Red River nine hundred out of the one thousand were fit for duty.

The fall of Vicksburg and Port Hudson gave the Federals complete control of the Mississippi, and, for the present, ended military operations along that river, with the exception of the abortive attempt of Lt. Gen. Holmes to surprise and capture Helena, Arkansas, a Federal, fortified, position on the Mississippi,[78] already mentioned in connection with Gen. [Samuel R.] Curtis's campaign of the year before. Since that time it had been kept up by the Federals as a point d'appui for the benefit of adventurers engaged in the cotton trade with the citizens of Arkansas, who, like a certain number that may be found in all countries, were willing enough to afford aid to the enemies of their country for a consideration. This mercenary spirit was not confined to Arkansas, and along the whole course of the Mississippi there were not wanting exam-

77. Dr. Beall was only twenty-nine years old when he organized this operation. He studied medicine at the University of Louisiana and in New York before the war and became one of Fort Worth's most accomplished surgeons and medical leaders after the war. See *History of Texas Together with a Biographical History of Tarrant and Parker Counties* (Chicago: Lewis Publishing Co., 1895), 532–34; *Transactions of the Southern Surgical and Gynecological Association,* 28 vols. (Birmingham, Ala.: Press of Caldwell Printing Co., 1887–1928), vol. 1: 79–85, 271–77.

78. See DeBlack, "1863: 'We Must Stand or Fight Alone,'" 79–84; Edwin C. Bearss, "The Battle of Helena, July 4, 1863," *Arkansas Historical Quarterly* 20 (Autumn 1961): 256–97.

ples of a shameful betrayal of the cause of the South by dishonest and disloyal men. The Federal armies in Virginia and the Carolinas, however found the people as a rule true to their principles, from which they could not be turned by intimidation, or promises of reward, but I am sorry to say that the population further west did not always give evidence of the possession of those stern virtues and Helena, Arkansas, became the centre of a profitable trade between Confederate cotton planters and Yankee cotton speculators;[79] and it was charged against Federal Generals, high in command, by northern newspapers, that they largely profited by this trade.

To break it up was the object of Gen. Holmes' attempt,[80] the failure of which added another example to the long list of disasters to the Confederate arms in attempting attack, or defense, of positions where the Federal superiority, or supremacy, upon the water could be asserted. In this instance, even if Gen. Holmes had succeeded, Helena would have been a useless acquisition, inasmuch as the Confederates would necessarily have abandoned the position as soon as acquired, and the Federals would have again have taken possession. As it was, it was a useless sacrifice of life, leading to defeat.

The same ruinous policy characterized the operations of Gen. Taylor in his attempts upon Milliken's Bend, Fort Butler, and other fortified positions upon the Mississippi. These actions, leading to no result if they had succeeded, wasted the Confederate strength and dispirited the troops.[81]

The next military event in the Trans-Mississippi Department

79. Walker had little patience for avaricious civilians and discovered more of them than expected west of the Mississippi River.

80. The major aim of the Confederate attack on Helena, to distract Federals from their pressure on Vicksburg, would have failed no matter the outcome of the battle because Vicksburg surrendered the same day.

81. Generals Walker and Taylor cooperated closely and cordially for most of their time together, but Taylor's frustration after Milliken's Bend had led him to disparage Walker's infantry for having an unreasonable "dread of gunboats." Walker protested, and Taylor later retracted his criticism, but Walker still regarded Taylor as unrealistic on the subject of gunboats. See Lowe, *Walker's Texas Division,* 102–4.

claiming our attention is the capture of Little Rock, Arkansas, by the Federal forces, and their occupation of the line of the Arkansas River.

Since the previous January when Sherman's forces under McClearnand [McClernand] had captured the garrison of the Post of the Arkansas, no serious attempt had been made by the Federal forces to extend their lines beyond Helena. It is true Gen. Blunt, early in '63, had occupied Fort Smith and the upper Arkansas without serious opposition, but these operations seemed to have no other purpose in view than to gain a position from which the Indian tribes inhabiting the territory west of Arkansas could be controlled, in the interest of the Federal cause.[82]

However the Federal government now determined to direct operations against the State looking to her conquest. To this end a force of some fifteen thousand men was appointed at Helena, and Gen. [Frederick] Steele, their commander, in the latter part of September, advanced toward Little Rock, the capital of the State.[83] White River, at all times navigable for steamers of considerable burden, was used for the transportation of the infantry, artillery and commissariat to Duval's Bluff, forty miles east of Little Rock.[84] From this point there is a railroad, the only one in the State, which, of course, the Confederates destroyed as they fell back toward the Arkansas River. A good deal of skirmishing took place as the Federal army advanced, but its superiority in numbers gradually pushed back the opposing forces, and finally it reached the Arkansas river and crossed it six miles below Little Rock. Gen. Sterling Price, now in command of the Confederates, hastily evacuating the place with his infantry, about seven thousand strong, and leaving Gen. Marmaduke, commanding the cavalry, about

82. Blunt's advances in Indian Territory and on the western border of Arkansas were in the spring and summer of 1863. See DeBlack, "1863: 'We Must Stand or Fall Alone,'" 85–88.

83. Major General Steele left Helena on August 10–11, not late September. A West Point classmate of Grant and Confederate General Franklin Gardner, Steele was given command of all Federal troops in Arkansas in late 1863 and ordered to flush Confederate forces out of the state. See Warner, *Generals in Blue*, 474–75; DeBlack, "1863: 'We Must Stand or Fall Alone,'" 90.

84. De Vall's Bluff is fifty-two road miles east of Little Rock.

twenty five thousand [*sic*] strong, to cover his retreat.[85] This officer performed his task in the most gallant manner, and in the frequent combats with the Federal cavalry sustained the reputation of the Confederate arms. In one of these encounters in the suburbs of Little Rock he captured a section of horse artillery and some prisoners.

The conduct of Gen. Price in evacuating Little Rock [on September 10] without attempting its defence was severely censured, and not without reason. It is true his forces in point of arms and equipment was greatly inferior to the enemy and numerically as three are to five, but a resolute and enterprising General with a river in his front which his enemy must cross to attack him would have contested the crossing.[86]

The retreat of the Confederate army, and the abandonment of the capital of the State produced feelings of profound discouragement in the public mind, and the incapacity of the Confederate leaders in that State became more and more apparent. The country lying between the Arkansas and Ouachita rivers, except the margins of the small streams, consists of unproductive pine forests, with a sparse population, and producing but little for the subsistence of an army. The valley of the Arkansas, which is of wonderful fertility and in a high state of cultivation, now being lost to the Confederates, Gen. Price was forced to retreat to the Ouachita, where he made his first stand, taking up a position at Arkadelphia, with his cavalry outposts at Benton, twenty miles south of Little Rock.[87]

During the autumn and winter of 1863 and 1864, the country lying between the Arkansas river and the Ouachita remained as a neutral ground and was the scene of almost weekly encounters between the cavalry of the two armies. What little the country pos-

85. Marmaduke had about 1,300 horsemen, not 25,000. Walker probably meant 2,500. See DeBlack, "1863: 'We Must Stand or Fall Alone,'" 91.

86. Price's 8,000 Confederates faced about 14,500 Federals, so Walker's estimate was close (DeBlack, "1863: 'We Must Stand or Fall Alone,'" 90, 92). Walker would have little reason to alter his opinion of Price's abilities in future operations.

87. Arkadadelphia is about seventy road miles southwest of Little Rock. Benton is twenty-five miles southwest of Little Rock.

sessed of provisions and forage was entirely consumed by friend and foe, and the miserable inhabitants left almost in a starving condition. But to the credit of the Federal General Steele it must be recorded that his treatment of the inhabitants of the country was invariably humane and considerate, presenting a striking contrast to the conduct of too many of the Federal leaders.

In western Louisiana it became apparent early in September that the Federal commander, Gen. Banks was meditating operations on a larger scale. Confederate scouts gave information of large numbers of troops and horses passing the Mississippi river, and New Orleans became the scene of active preparations by land and water for operations on a large scale. By the light of intercepted correspondence it afterwards appeared that the expedition had but little reference to purely military or political results, but was, in fact, undertaken for the sake of the immense booty in cotton, which, it was hoped, would fall into the hands of the Federal commander. The traitorous Confederate agent of this Cotton Bureau had a secret understanding with Gen. Banks that the whole of the cotton crop of Western Louisiana would, through his instrumentality, be placed at Niblett's Bluff on the Sabine [River], to which point the river is navigable for steamers entering the mouth of the river from the Gulf of Mexico from which it is distant about forty miles.[88] According to the intercepted correspondence above referred to, McKee, the cotton agent of the Confederate Government, promised Banks a booty of forty thousand bales by the month of October.[89] To secure this rich booty was the object of the operations which followed.

It seems to have been Gen. Banks' desire to cover the real purpose of the expedition, namely, the acquisition of cotton under the pretext of the invasion of Texas, and the permanent occupation of that State.[90] The double purpose was perhaps in view, but it is dif-

88. Niblett's Bluff is about 120 road miles northeast of Houston, on the Texas-Louisiana border.

89. Andrew W. McKee was the official who had been tried for treason, espionage, and trafficking with the enemy but then jumped bail and disappeared, much to Walker's irritation.

90. In fact, Banks did have other motives for his operation: to warn France against meddling with the Confederates; to establish a pro-Union state govern-

ficult to believe that the serious invasion of Texas was intended by a long overland route, destitute of supplies, and in many places at this season of the year of water for distances of thirty and forty miles,[91] whereas by means of his unlimited steam transportation the Federal commander could land his army, without suffering and without loss, on any part of the coast within fifty miles of Houston, and, from a secure base of operations and supply upon the Gulf of Mexico, march at his leisure to the almost unopposed possession of the heart of the State.

In order to secure a base of supplies for his army, at the same time to take possession of the cotton, at Niblett's Bluff, Gen. Banks, early in September, dispatched Gen. [William B.] Franklin with a division of infantry embarked upon steamers and escorted by gunboats to the mouth of the Sabine.[92] The entrance to the river was guarded by a field work upon which was mounted three thirty two pounder smooth bores, and one twenty four pounder howitzer, and a garrison of forty seven men. Fortunately for the Confederates the depth of water on the bar, seven feet, permitted only two of the Federal gun boats to enter the river, while the fleet of transports awaited outside for what was thought the easy capture of the Confederate position. The result, the capture of the two gunboats, with four hundred and thirty prisoners, by the Confederates, was so unexpected and discouraging that no other attempt was made by Gen. Franklin, and he immediately returned with his entire force to New Orleans.[93]

---

ment in Texas; and to ship Texas cotton to idle New York and New England textile mills. Walker believed profiteering was the primary driver of Banks's operations. See Richard Lowe, *The Texas Overland Expedition of 1863* (1996; rpt., Abilene, Texas: McWhiney Foundation Press, 1998), 15–20.

91. A march from New Orleans to Houston, about 350 road miles, would require Banks to traverse long stretches of barely settled coastal prairies that could not supply an army's needs.

92. Franklin, first in his class of 1843 at West Point, had commanded a Federal division in Virginia in 1862. Accused of poor performance at the Battle of Fredericksburg, he was transferred to the Trans-Mississippi theater in 1863. See Mark Snell, *From First to Last: The Life of William B. Franklin* (Bronx, N.Y.: Fordham University Press, 2002).

93. Confederates compared this embarrassing defeat for Federal forces to the ancient Battle of Thermopylae. See Alwyn Barr, "Sabine Pass, Battle of," in Tyler

While Franklin was engaged in this profitless attack, a corps of Federal troops, numbering about seventeen thousand men of all arms was pushed forward [in September and October 1863] under Banks in person along the Têche as far as Vermillionville, the point of divergence of the roads leading to Alexandria on Red River and Niblett's Bluff on the Sabine. Here Banks was soon joined by Franklin's discomforted division, raising his strength to nearly twenty two thousand men, of whom probably twenty five hundred were cavalry and mounted infantry, and eight hundred artillery, with forty eight guns.

Banks now returned to New Orleans, and though Franklin was left in the immediate command in the field, the former continued to control the movements of the army by means of telegraph and signals. Some of his dispatches to Franklin were captured by the Confederates, affording ample proof of this fact. The Confederate force opposed to this formidable Federal column was six thousand four hundred infantry, viz: Walker's division of Texans, four thousand, and [Alfred] Mouton's division of Louisianians, twenty four hundred, each division having four batteries, or thirty two pieces of field artillery, of which one third were rifled. The Confederate cavalry commanded by Brig. Gen. [Tom] Green, although amounting fully to two thousand men, were badly armed, and but little drilled or disciplined.

With his vast superiority of force it was supposed that if Texas no longer formed the objective point of Federal operations that Franklin would, at least, endeavor to cover his failure by the éclat of a successful advance to Red River. In fact this seems to have been at one time his intention as well as could be judged from the marching and counter marching that characterized the Federal movements. Eventually the bulk of the Federal army reached the town of Opelousas compelling the Confederates to fall back, towards Alexandria.[94] Their [the Confederates'] superiority in cav-

---

et al., eds., *New Handbook of Texas* 5: 745; Edward T. Cotham Jr., *Sabine Pass: The Confederacy's Thermopylae* (Austin: University of Texas Press, 2004).

94. Opelousas is about sixty-five road miles west of Baton Rouge and equal distance southeast of Alexandria.

alry, however, enabled them to encamp in sight of the enemy's campfires, and to prevent the devastation of the country by small foraging parties. The Federal army from this point retraced its steps towards the Gulf of Mexico, and on the morning of the 28th. of October were found to have withdrawn from the town of Opelousas, which was at once reoccupied by the Confederates under Gen. Green, with three regiments of Texas infantry and two brigades of cavalry under Brig. Generals [Arthur P.] Bagley [Bagby] and [James P.] Majors.[95]

Following up the rear of the Federal column on the next morning [November 3, 1863,] Gen. Green overtook the rear of the Federal army consisting of a division of infantry, two squadrons of cavalry, and two light batteries, under Brig. Gen. [Stephen G.] Burbridge, encamped twelve miles south of Opelousas at a small stream called the Barbeux [Bourbeau].[96] Here Gen. Green attacked them with his infantry with such impetuosity that the Federals were completely defeated, losing in killed and wounded and prisoners over seven hundred men, of whom six hundred were prisoners, besides a section of field artillery. The Confederate cavalry took but little part in the engagement save to bring in the prisoners when the rout became general.[97] Franklin, who was at the time at the town of Vermillionville, twelve miles south, with his main army, immediately returned with the greater part of his force, but the Confederates, having secured their prisoners and removed their killed and wounded which did not exceed sixty, had retired

95. Colonel Bagby was a graduate of the U.S. Military Academy, class of 1852. James P. Major, West Point class of 1856, had served with the famed Second U.S. Cavalry Regiment before the Civil War and fought in a Missouri State Guard unit at Wilson's Creek. See Warner, *Generals in Gray*, 24–25, 209–10.

96. Generals Walker and Green did not realize that the Federals at Bayou Bourbeau were only part of a division. Burbridge, a Kentucky lawyer before the war and a veteran of Shiloh, Arkansas Post, and Vicksburg, commanded about 1,800 men, including five hundred cavalry and eight guns. See Warner, *Generals in Blue*, 54–55; Lowe, *Texas Overland Expedition*, 65–68.

97. Two of the three Confederate infantry regiments (the Eleventh and Eighteenth Texas) were part of Walker's division. The third, the Fifteenth Texas, usually served in Mouton's brigade. Walker was happy to attribute Confederate success that day to the infantry.

to Opelousas, and the Federal commander finding pursuit useless, resumed his retrograde march and returned to Berwick's Bay, and, finally, to New Orleans.[98]

This brilliant little affair closed military operations in western Louisiana for the year, but the belligerent armies kept up during the autumn and winter a system of pickets and cavalry scouting into each other's lines that led to many small encounters marked by courage and daring on both sides, but having no military results. It should be mentioned, however, that the retrograde movement of Franklin's army was hastened, if not inaugurated, by the Confederate blockade of the Mississippi by the forces under General Walker. While Green was watching the movements of the Federal army in the Atluchipas country,[99] Major Gen. Walker, with his own division and that of Gen. Mouton, crossed the Atchafalaya upon bridges constructed of "coolers" from neighboring sugar houses, and dried logs, and with thirty pieces of field artillery established himself near the mouth of Red River,[100] and for several weeks rendered the navigation of the Mississippi, except by iron clad gun boats, so hazardous as to threaten the Federal army with famine, its supplies reaching them from there north by way of the Mississippi River.[101]

However before the Federal army could change its front so as to reopen its line of supply the Confederates were forced to retire west of the Atchafalaya by the rapid rise of its waters, which threatened the destruction of its bridges, which would have left them at the

98. Lowe, *Walker's Texas Division*, 136–45; Lowe, *Texas Overland Expedition*, 80–104; David C. Edmonds, *Yankee Autumn in Acadiana: A Narrative of the Great Texas Overland Expedition Through Southwestern Louisiana, October–December 1863* (Lafayette, La.: Acadiana Press, 1979), 274–95.

99. Walker's use of the word "Atluchipas" apparently jumbled two Louisiana geographic terms, Atchafalaya (for the river) and Attakapas (for an Indian tribe). He was probably referring to the region of south Louisiana from Brashear City on the south to Vermilionville on the north.

100. Coolers were troughs used to cool molasses in the sugar-making process. Walker adapted them into pontoons.

101. Although Walker's division did not completely "blockade" the river, the Texans certainly interfered with Union shipping on the Mississippi in the winter of 1863–64. Confederate field guns and rifle fire swept the muddy water and severely damaged several vessels. See Lowe, *Walker's Texas Division*, 150–56.

mercy of the enemy's overwhelming forces. To understand this it must be borne in mind that this stream is one of the mouths of Red River, which breaking off from it some ten miles before its entrance into the Mississippi runs due south and almost parallel to that river, and falls into an arm of the Gulf of Mexico called Atchafalaya Bay. It is a stream of an average width of two hundred yards, has a swift current and [is] navigable for steamers.

CHAPTER 3.

Military Operations
West of the Mississippi during the Year 1864

To enable the reader more clearly to understand what follows it will [be] useful to bear in mind the strength and relative situation of the Federal and Confederate armies at the opening of the season for active operations in the Spring of '64. As has already been said Gen. Franklin [*should be* Frederick] Steele occupied Little Rock and the valley of the Arkansas, and, of course, the whole country north of that river, with a force of about twelve thousand infantry and two thousand five hundred cavalry. Gen. Price, commanding the Confederate forces in that State, with six thousand infantry and three thousand cavalry, occupied the line of the Ouachita River, drawing his supplies from the valley of the Red River and the lower Ouachita. The main Federal army of the South west under Gen. Banks was concentrated at New Orleans, with outpost garrisons as far west on the Gulf of Mexico as Berwick's Bay, and north as Plaquimine [*sic*], on the Mississippi.[1]

During the winter of 1863–4 it became known to the Confederates that heavy reinforcements were descending the Mississippi to New Orleans, and that that city was the scene of preparations on a grand scale for the campaign of the Spring. But whether Texas, or Louisiana, was to be the theatre of war could only be conjectured. The Confederate commander in western La. [Richard Taylor], however, was well convinced that Banks' attempt of the previous year would be repeated, and the rich valley of the Red River was the coveted prize. This conjecture, however, met with an appar-

---

1. Berwick Bay, eighty air miles southwest of New Orleans, connected Brashear City to the Gulf of Mexico. Plaquimine is eighty air miles northwest (upriver) from New Orleans. Once again, it appears that Walker was not fully aware of the Federal army-navy operation in late 1863 that placed U.S. Army garrisons along the lower Texas coast down to the Rio Grande. See Townsend, *Yankee Invasion of Texas.*

ent contradiction in the month of January when a numerous fleet of armed vessels and transports appeared off the coast of Texas, west of Matagorda Bay [on the Texas coast, about 100 miles southwest of Houston], and landed a force of ten thousand men under Gen. Heron, which, except the capture of the small fort Esperanza, at the entrance of Matagorda Bay, effected nothing, and after a stay of some two weeks at Lavaca, Indianola, and on the peninsular formed by Matorga [*sic*] Bay and the Gulf, like the expedition of the year before under Franklin, re-embarked and returned to New Orleans.[2] This movement upon Texas, however, made it necessary to strengthen the Confederate forces under Gen. Magruder in that State, and the whole of the Texas cavalry under Gen. Green marched hastily from Western La. for that purpose.

If the valley of Red River was to be the scene of the Federal operations it was evident that the naval forces on the Mississippi would bear an important part. Therefore, early in the winter, the attention of Gen. Taylor was seriously directed to the erection of such fortifications on its banks, and the placing of such obstructions in the channel of Red River as his limited means afforded. The point selected for this purpose was about fifty miles from the confluence of that river and the Mississippi, and twenty miles [upstream] from the mouth of Black or Ouichita [Ouachita].[3] The immediate topography of this point known as Fort De Russy was most unfavorable for its successful defense, being commanded by a range of hills too extensive to be held by a force of less than ten thousand men, and which once in the possession of the enemy rendered Fort De Russy untenable.[4] The obstructions [in the river] which should

2. Walker, with no personal knowledge of the war along the Texas coast, again confused two different operations around Matagorda Bay. A small U.S. naval force briefly captured the fort, seventy-five air miles northeast of Corpus Christi on the Texas coast, in October 1862 and then quickly abandoned it. A larger infantry operation, in November 1863, captured the installation and held it until June 1864. In neither case was Federal Major General Francis J. Herron involved. See Townsend, *Yankee Invasion of Texas*, 28–31; Arnold, "Fort Esperanza."

3. The defensive work Walker referred to, Fort De Russy, was three miles north of Marksville, Louisiana, on the right bank of the Red River.

4. The range of hills Walker referred to was only a gentle rise and did not play a role in the eventual capture of the fort. See Steven M. Mayeux, *Earthen Walls,*

have been auxiliary to the fort were placed six miles below it, thus leaving the enemy the opportunity to remove them at his leisure. These defects, as will be seen, were fatal.

The garrison of Fort De Russy consisted of three hundred infantry and three companies of heavy artillery, manning twelve guns of large caliber, the whole commanded by Lt. Col. [William] Byrd.[5] The line of the Atchafalaya, twenty five miles nearer the Mississippi was held by Major Gen. Walker, commanding three brigades of infantry, numbering in all thirty eight hundred muskets. One of the Brigades, commanded by Brig. Gen. [William R.] Scurry,[6] occupied Simmsport, on the Atchafalaya, the other two were encamped at Marksville, twenty miles west [*actually* northwest]. This force was thought entirely sufficient to cover Fort De Russy against any attempt of the enemy less than corps d'armees, although a serious danger would menace an inferior covering force from the fact that Fort De Russy was situated upon an island from which there was no exit except by a bridge which the enemy, if in superior force, must necessarily command.[7]

On the evening of the 12th of March Major Gen. A. J. Smith entered the mouth of Red River with a fleet of gun boats, and twenty seven transports, and turning into the Atchafalaya disembarked

---

Iron Men: Fort DeRussy, Louisiana, and the Defense of Red River (Knoxville: University of Tennessee Press, 2007); e-mail from Steven M. Mayeux to Richard Lowe, July 12, 2010, in possession of the latter.

5. William Byrd, born into the famous Byrd family of Virginia, was a graduate of the Virginia Military Institute and the law department at the University of Virginia. His grandchildren included the famous polar aviator and explorer Richard Byrd and the powerful U.S. Senator Harry Byrd. See Thomas W. Cutrer, "Byrd, William," in Tyler et al., eds., *New Handbook of Texas* 1: 875.

6. Scurry, a Tennessee native, had served in a Texas unit in the war with Mexico and had been a member of the Texas secession convention. A veteran of the New Mexico campaign and the recapture of Galveston, he had been given command of a brigade in Walker's division a few months earlier. A West Texas county is named for him. See Thomas W. Cutrer, "Scurry, William Read," in Tyler et al., eds., *New Handbook of Texas* 5: 946.

7. Walker meant that the fort was surrounded by the Red River on the north, swamps to the west and east, and two bayous on the far side of high prairie land on the south. Only one bridge, about ten miles southwest of the fort, connected this "island" to the rest of the state.

his forces consisting of the 16th Corps d'Armée, lately returned from Sherman's raid upon central Mississippi, to which was added a portion of Banks' army proper, from New Orleans, which joined him at the mouth of Red River, raising his entire force to about sixteen thousand men of all arms.[8]

Some skirmishing took place between the Federals and Confederates at the landing, but the small force of Gen. Scurry was forced to fall back the same night to Bayou de Glaise, ten miles to the west. The next morning Gen. Walker came up with the brigades of [Horace] Randal and [James M.] Hawes,[9] and having made a personal reconnaissance of the advancing army of Gen. Smith, and satisfying himself as to its strength, after skirmishing with the advance for some hours, was forced to withdraw and leave the garrison of Fort De Russy to its fate. It was necessary either to adopt this cruel alternative, or to shut his division up on an island and share the fate of Fort De Russy.[10]

Although its capture ultimately was inevitable, Col. Byrd was instructed to hold out to the last extremity, as its evacuation would enable the enemy to push his whole force up the [Red] river by means of his steam transports and iron clad gun boats, and thus anticipate the Confederates at Alexandria, and by cutting off their retreat toward Nachitoches and Shreveport throw the Confeder-

8. Brigadier General Andrew J. Smith, a member of the West Point class of 1838, had served on the western frontier before the Civil War and had commanded divisions at Arkansas Post and in the Vicksburg campaign. He brought about 10,000 troops from Sherman's command at Vicksburg to capture Fort De Russy and drive up the Red River with Banks. See Warner, *Generals in Blue,* 454–55.

9. Colonel Horace Randal, a graduate of the U.S. Military Academy's class of 1854, had fought on the Apache frontier before the war and led a Texas cavalry regiment before assuming command of a brigade in Walker's division in late 1862. A county in West Texas is named for him. James M. Hawes, a member of the West Point class of 1845, had fought in the Mexican War, studied tactics at a French cavalry school, and served in the western theater of the war before taking command of a brigade in Walker's division in late 1862. See Bruce S. Allardice, *More Generals in Gray* (Baton Rouge: Louisiana State University Press, 1995), 192–93; Johansson, *Peculiar Honor*; Warner, *Generals in Gray,* 128–29.

10. Walker had expressed the same deep regret (about abandoning the soldiers in the fort) at the time of these events. He found the necessity "mortifying." See *Official Records* 34, pt. 1: 599.

ate army back into the desert country between Red River and the Sabine.[11]

On the afternoon of the 13th Fort De Russy was invested, and from the inherent defects of its situation already alluded to it was found indefensible. Notwithstanding the garrison made a gallant resistance, forcing the enemy to take it by assault, in which he suffered heavily from the infantry, but the artillery could not be used, as from hills which commanded it the gunners could not man their guns, all of which were in barbette.[12]

Combined with this movement Gen. Banks, five days previously, had moved from Berwick's Bay with ten thousand infantry and six thousand cavalry and mounted riflemen, taking the road pursued by him the previous year, which leads along the Têche, through Opelousas towards Alexandria on Red River, which was to be the point of concentration of the Federal forces for the conquest of western Louisiana and Texas. The position occupied by Gen. Walker's forces covering Fort De Russy, as has already been mentioned, was insular, and the rapid advance of Banks' column to seize the only outlet, rendered the position of that officer [Walker] critical in the extreme, and it was only by the most rapid movement that he was enabled to extricate his division from this cul de sac and gain the high road on Bayou Boeuf before its closure by the arrival of Banks' overwhelming force.[13]

In the meantime Mouton's infantry division consisting of [Henry] Gray's brigade of Louisiana infantry, and [Camille Armand] Polignac's brigade of Texans, formed a junction with Walker's division, Major General Taylor assuming command of the whole.[14]

11. Walker's reference to "desert country" was not literal. Large stretches of the sparsely settled piney woods of northwest Louisiana were generally devoid of agricultural produce and adequate water supplies.

12. "In barbette" meant that Confederate artillery pieces were located at the top of the fort's parapet, without the protection of a casemate. The best study of the capture of De Russy is Mayeux, *Earthen Walls, Iron Men*.

13. The "high road" referred to the higher ground near Cheneyville, about ten miles west of the "island" around Fort De Russy.

14. Colonel Henry Gray, a graduate of South Carolina College, had been a lawyer and state legislator in both Mississippi and Louisiana before the war. Camille Armand Jules Marie, Prince de Polignac, was a member of a French noble

The fall of Fort De Russy had now removed the only obstruction to the navigation of Red River, and placed it in the power of Gen. A. J. Smith to push forward his army corps to Alexandria by steamers,[15] and to occupy the road leading toward Nachitoches and Shreveport which passes within a half day's march for Alexandria, thus forcing Gen. Taylor back in the pine desert lying between the Red River and the Sabine, which being entirely destitute of subsistence and forage would have been its destruction as an organized army. Also an engagement against overwhelming odds was equally hazardous. The want of prompt action, or perhaps of local knowledge of terrain on the part of the Federal commander, saved the Confederate army, which was permitted by force[d] marches to gain the high road west of Alexandria, and could now pursue its march westward through a country from which subsistence could be drawn, until such time as reinforcements could enable it to turn and contest with some chance of success the progress of the enemy. These reinforcements were now hastening from Texas and Arkansas.[16]

On the 16th and 17th of March the columns of Banks and Smith formed a junction at Alexandria raising their combined force to an effective [*sic*] of quite twenty five thousand infantry and six to seven thousand cavalry or mounted infantry.

---

family. Educated in Paris, he had served in the French army during the Crimean War and in the western theater of the Civil War before taking command of a brigade of Texans in the Trans-Mississippi Department in 1863. He later led a French division in the Franco-Prussian War. See Warner, *Generals in Gray*, 115, 241–42; Jeff Kinard, *Lafayette of the South: Prince Camille de Polignac and the American Civil War* (College Station: Texas A&M University Press, 2001).

15. Although Walker and others usually referred to A. J. Smith's command as the Federal Sixteenth Corps, it was in fact a detachment of two divisions from the Sixteenth Corps. See Boatner, *Civil War Dictionary*, 196.

16. The reinforcements included 2,500 cavalry moving east from Texas and 4,500 Missouri and Arkansas infantry moving south from Arkansas. See E. Kirby Smith, "The Defense of Red River," in Johnson and Buel, eds., *Battles and Leaders* 4: 370–72; Ludwell H. Johnson, *Red River Campaign: Politics and Cotton in the Civil War* (Baltimore: Johns Hopkins Press, 1958), 119; Richard Taylor, *Destruction and Reconstruction: Personal Experiences of the Civil War* (1879; rpt. with a new introduction by T. Michael Parrish, New York: Da Capo Press, 1995), 162.

The Federal plan of campaign contemplated the cooperation of the forces in Arkansas under Gen. Steele. Consequently this General was already in motion [from Little Rock toward Shreveport] with twelve thousand infantry and two thousand five hundred cavalry, whose horses, however, were in bad condition. To oppose this force Gen. Price had now nothing but the cavalry of Marmaduke and [James F.] Fagan, and a brigade of mounted volunteers under [Richard M.] Gano, and a regiment of half civilized Cherokee Indians under Col. Stan Waitie [Stand Watie], numbering in all about six thousand men.[17] Of course this badly organized and undisciplined body of horsemen could offer no effectual check to Steele's advance. The country, however, through which the Federals were passing being utterly destitute of subsistence and forage, it was necessary to draw his supplies from the Arkansas river over wretched roads. The danger of the capture of these supply trains made it necessary to employ so large a proportion of his infantry force in escorting supply trains from his base of supply on the Arkansas river that this, in some measure, neutralized his vast superiority of force, and of itself would have accounted for the tardiness of his movements. Besides this he was marching through a destitute country whose roads, never good, were now by the Spring rains rendered next to impossible. The bridges, not swept away by the floods, were, of course, destroyed by the Confederates; the front, rear, and flanks of his army harrassed [*sic*], often at the same time, by Price's irregular cavalry and mounted riflemen, accustomed from infancy to this mode of warfare; the necessity of deploying his whole infantry force frequently more than once during a day's march to force some advantageous position obstinately held by Price, all conspired to retard the movements of the Federal army, and give the Confederates opportunity to throw their whole remaining force upon Banks before Steele's column could possibly

17. Fagan and Gano were both Kentuckians in their mid-thirties. Fagan was a planter in Arkansas; Gano, a physician in Texas. Both had served in the western theater before being assigned to the Trans-Mississippi. Stand Watie was a famous Cherokee leader whose Cherokee regiment had fought at Wilson's Creek and Pea Ridge. See Warner, *Generals in Gray,* 85–86, 96, 327–28; Frank Cunningham, *General Stand Watie's Confederate Indians* (Norman: University of Oklahoma Press, 1998).

afford the former any positive co-operation. If, on the one hand, Banks was defeated, Steele was not sufficiently strong to advance alone[;] if, on the other hand, Banks should defeat Taylor, Steele's defeat would not retrieve the disaster, or save the valley of the Red River and the whole of Western Louisiana and Eastern Texas from Federal invasion and conquest. It will thus be seen that the whole Federal plan of campaign was based upon the vicious system of operating upon an immense circumference, while the Confederates operated upon interior lines. The result proved the advantage of the latter.[18]

While these events were transpiring in Arkansas, and while Steele was slowly making his way to Camden, on the Ouachita River [in southern Arkansas], which he reached about the 3rd of April, Banks was making vast preparations at Alexandria for his advance westward. A fleet of fifteen gun boats, some of them formidable iron clads, under Admiral Porter, had already passed the Falls at that point [Alexandria], and in addition a fleet of steamers for the transportation of munitions of war and supplies of all kinds, and, when necessary, his infantry, was in attendance.[19] About the 24th. of March this grand armament commenced its movement by land and water, the ironclads taking the lead on water, followed by gun boats of less powers of resistance, and following them were the steam transports. As the road westward, as far as Nachitoches, follows the right bank of the river, the fleet proceeded <u>para passa</u> [*pari passu,* or, at the same rate] with the

18. The "immense circumference" included Steele's advance from Little Rock on the north, Banks's movement from New Orleans on the south, and A. J. Smith's assistance from Vicksburg on the east. The straight-line distance from Little Rock to New Orleans was 350 miles; from Little Rock to Vicksburg, 190 miles; and from Vicksburg to New Orleans, 170 miles. Meanwhile, the Confederates operated between these points and thus moved their men more quickly over shorter distances (i.e., interior lines).

19. The U.S. naval fleet included thirteen heavy ironclads, four tinclads, five other gunboats, troop transports, supply ships, and hospital ships—altogether, ninety vessels carrying 210 heavy naval guns, the largest war fleet ever assembled on western rivers. See Thomas O. Selfridge, "The Navy in the Red River," in Johnson and Buel, eds., *Battles and Leaders* 4: 366; Gary D. Joiner and Charles E. Vetter, "The Union Naval Expedition on the Red River, March 12–May 22, 1864," *Civil War Regiments* 4 (no. 2, 1994): 26–67.

forces on land in such manner as to co-operate in case of necessity. General Taylor having no cavalry, and having instructions
from Gen. E. K. Smith not to risk a general engagement until reinforcement should reach him, offered no resistance to the Federal army which reached Nachitoches, a town on Red River, seventy miles from Alexandria, on the 29th of March. At this point
the road westward leading through a pine forest, interrupted here
and there by inconsiderable farms and openings, takes a more interior direction, but still one on the whole parallel to Red River,
from which it is never distant more than fifteen miles, and to be
reached at two or three points only by lateral roads. At Shreveport
the road again touches the river. Some days were consumed at this
point [i.e., Natchitoches] by the Federal commander in establishing depots and hospitals and on the third of April Banks resumed
his march with the 13th and 19th Army Corps and his cavalry,
dispatching Major Gen. A. J. Smith with the 16th and a portion of
the 17th Army Corps up the river on transports, escorted by Admiral Porter's fleet—the two columns to unite at Shreveport.

In the meantime considerable reinforcements of horsemen
under Gen. Green were reaching Taylor from Texas, and henceforward there was constant skirmishing between the cavalry of
the two armies, in which batteries of horse artillery on each side
took a conspicuous part. The superior qualities of the Texas horsemen, accustomed to this irregular mode of warfare in these encounters, generally asserted itself, Green only falling back before
the advance in force of Banks' infantry.

Taylor had now reached Mansfield, forty eight miles [north]
west of Nachitoches. To this point there was but a single road that
Banks could pursue. Once beyond it, however, he would brave
[i.e., have] the choice of three. Thus, should Taylor attempt to
guard one he might be seriously compromised by a rapid movement of the enemy upon another. Beyond Mansfield the enemy's
advance could not be disputed with prudence, short of the point
of junction of these various routes, which was almost in the suburbs of Shreveport, where the enemy's entire army would be re-
united and resistance to which would be impossible. General Taylor, therefore, wisely determined to try the hazards of a general
engagement in front of Mansfield, although the [infantry] rein-

forcements from Arkansas had not yet reached him. It is true that they had reached Shreveport as early as the 25th of March, fourteen days previous, where, under one pretext or another, they were detained by Gen. E. K. Smith, whose orders to Gen. Taylor were not to hazard a general engagement until these reinforcements had joined him. That Gen. Taylor did not intend to disobey these instructions seems certain from the fact that on the afternoon of the 7th the infantry of Walker and Mouton were ordered to pass [north] through Mansfield and encamp seven miles beyond. But the information that A. J. Smith was ascending Red River with the 16th Army Corps reached Taylor on the night of the 7th and determined him to bring on an engagement the next day in front of [south of] Mansfield with the forces there under his orders.

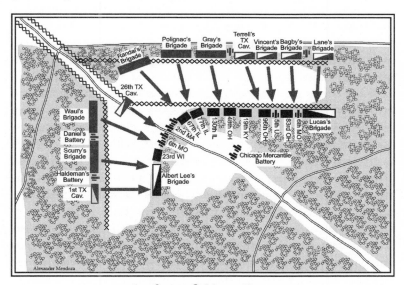

Battle of Mansfield, April 8, 1864

On the morning of the 8th of April Walker and Mouton retraced their steps through Mansfield, and took up a favorable position three miles in advance [south] of the town. In the meantime Green with three brigades of Texas cavalry was gallantly disputing the advance of the enemy, foot by foot. Walker[']s and Mouton's divisions had scarcely completed their line of battle, the first [Walker] on the right, the second [Mouton] on the left, when Green's cavalry was driven back upon them by the advance of the enemy in force. Green seeing himself supported by the Confederates in line of battle, gallantly assumed the offensive and attacked with his dismounted cavalry the right of the enemy's line of battle, which was now formed. The Confederate line occupied the margin of a pine forest, with a field of some half mile in width in its front, its left being thrown somewhat to the front as upon the horn of a crescent. Up to this moment the Confederate commander was undecided as to the propriety of bringing on a general engagement[20] until the obstinacy of Green's resistance, now supported by Mouton, who advanced without orders, had resulted in the capture of a Federal field battery and hundreds of prisoners, determined to take advantage of this partial success and advance his whole line.[21] Walker's division, impatient of delay, now moved rapidly to the front in échelon of brigades, with instructions to attack the enemy with the bayonet. This order was executed in the most gallant style. Moving across a field which lay in their front, and exposed to heavy fire of artillery and musketry at a support arms it attacked the enemy lining the woods beyond with such impetuosity that his line was instantly broken and he fled in the utmost disorder, pursued so closely by the Confederates that every attempt to reform was frustrated by their rapid advance. The flight was mostly through an open pine forest, and there was but one narrow country road, along which they had advanced. This flight and pursuit was kept up for two miles and a half when the trains of the cavalry division and a part of that of the 13th. Army Corps was reached. Here the blockade of the road was complete, and artillery, ambulances, and vehicles of every description were found

20. Walker, with his division on the right of the Confederate line, was not privy to the thinking of Taylor, near Mouton's division on the left, who was determined to engage the Federals. Taylor's intention, he later reported, was "to fight a general engagement" that day. See *Official Records* 34, pt. 1: 563; Taylor, *Destruction and Reconstruction,* 162, 163.

21. Although there were a few spontaneous eruptions of gunfire on the Confederate left before the main battle, Mouton's division advanced only when ordered forward by Taylor. In his report on the battle, Taylor wrote, "I ordered Mouton to open the attack from the left." See *Official Records* 34, pt. 1: 564.

abandoned, a majority with the harnessed animals attached, except the artillery upon which gunners had made their escape.[22] In the meantime the 19th. Army Corps had been hurried to the front, and taking up a strong position on an eminence one mile beyond the captured train, with a large field in front, forming by its gradual slope a natural glacis.[23]

Behind this line the routed 13th. Corps and cavalry took refuge, and after a gallant attempt of Walker's division, supported by a portion of Mouton's, to carry the hill, darkness put an end to the conflict, leaving the enemy in its [the hill's] possession.[24]

The Confederate troops, much scattered in this long pursuit through the forest, were reorganized during the night and lay upon their armes [*sic*] on the field of battle, ready to take up the pursuit or to renew the battle at to-morrow's dawn. At eleven o'clock at night, however, it was known to Gen. Walker, who was left in command, that the enemy had left his immediate front and continued his retreat.[25]

The substantial fruits of the victory were twenty two pieces of field artillery with their caissons complete, two hundred and twenty new army wagons, laden with subsistence, ammunition and baggage, with their horses and mules, thirty ambulances, and thirty five hundred prisoners, and the rout of Banks' whole

22. The Federals' chaotic retreat through the pine forest was one of the most vivid memories of the battle to those who survived. A Maine veteran of the rout at First Manassas (Bull Run) claimed that the panic in the woods near Mansfield was worse. See Henry N. Fairbanks, "The Red River Expedition of 1864," in *War Papers Read Before the Commandery of the State of Maine, Military Order of the Loyal Legion of the United States,* 4 vols. (1898–1915; rpt., Wilmington, N.C.: Broadfoot, 1992), vol. 1: 182.

23. A glacis is a gentle incline of ground in front of a fortified position.

24. The Confederates retained control of a stream at the foot of the hill, the only source of water for miles around. See Johnson, *Red River Campaign,* 139.

25. Walker was in command because Taylor had returned to Mansfield to arrange care for the wounded and to meet the Missouri and Arkansas infantry reinforcements just arriving from the north. Banks began his retreat at around 10 p.m. because fresh reinforcements were too far away to arrive before morning and because his men and animals had no water. See Taylor, *Destruction and Reconstruction,* 164; Johnson, *Red River Campaign,* 146–47; Gary Dillard Joiner, *One Damn Blunder from Beginning to End: The Red River Campaign of 1864* (Wilmington, Del.: Scholarly Resources, 2003), 107.

army. The Confederate loss was less than one thousand killed and wounded.[26] Amongst the former was the gallant Brig. Gen. Alfred Mouton, who was treacherously murdered by five Federal soldiers after they had surrendered.[27]

The forces engaged on the side of the Confederates [consisted] of Walker's Division, three thousand eight hundred strong, Mouton's Division, twenty four hundred or six thousand two hundred infantry, and four brigades of Cavalry amounting to three thousand seven hundred men, of whom one half only were engaged, and about forty five pieces of field artillery which took but little part in the battle owing to the wooded nature of the field and the rapidity with which all the Federal positions were carried.

The forces of the enemy present and taking part in the engagement consisted in the 13th and 19th Army Corps, the cavalry and mounted riflemen under Gen. [Albert L.] Lee,[28] with their respective parks of artillery, amounting to probably seventy pieces, although owing to the nature of the roads more than that captured by the Confederates may not have been actually engaged. That seems to have been the case from the fact that the last position taken up by the enemy was undefended by artillery although eminently suited to its use. The whole Federal force actually engaged, or in reserve on the battle field, could not have been less than

26. Estimates of Federal losses in materiel varied between Taylor's and Banks's accounts, possibly because U.S. Army figures did not include property lost by civilians accompanying the Union column. In either set of figures, the damages were considerable: at least twenty pieces of artillery, 150 to 200 wagons, thousands of small arms, and a thousand horses and mules. See Taylor, *Destruction and Reconstruction*, 164; Johnson, *Red River Campaign*, 140–41.

27. Mouton, according to some men who were on the field, was killed by Federal prisoners who had thrown down their arms but picked them up when they noticed that Mouton was alone. See Arthur W. Bergeron Jr., ed., *The Civil War Reminiscences of Major Silas T. Grisamore, C.S.A.* (Baton Rouge: Louisiana State University Press, 1993), 148; Sarah A. Dorsey, *Recollections of Henry Watkins Allen, Brigadier-General, Confederate States Army, Ex-Governor of Louisiana* (New Orleans: J. A. Gresham, 1866), 261–62; Arceneaux, *Acadian General Alfred Mouton*, 132.

28. Brigadier General Albert L. Lee, born and educated in New York State, was a Kansas lawyer before the war. A veteran of the Vicksburg campaign and chief of the Federal cavalry routed at Bayou Bourbeau, he was commander of Banks's cavalry division at Mansfield. See Warner, *Generals in Blue*, 278.

twenty five thousand men of all arms, while that of the Confederates, as will be seen by the foregoing did not exceed ten thousand
five hundred.[29]

The Battle of Pleasant Hill

The following morning the reinforcements from Arkansas, under
the command of Brig. Gen. [Thomas J.] Churchill, reached the battle field, and the whole Confederate force took up the pursuit of the
Federal army. Since early dawn two regiments of cavalry, under
Col. George Baylor, had been harrassing [*sic*] the enemy's rear and
sending in considerable detachments of prisoners.[30] Later in the
day Gen. Green, with the entire Confederate cavalry overtook the
Federal army at Pleasant Hill, which was reinforced by the 16th
Army Corps and a part of the 17th, under A. J. Smith. This force
had disembarked at Blair's Landing on Red River, and had joined
the main army by one of the cross roads already mentioned.[31]

Anticipating the Confederate pursuit Banks had taken up a
strong position at Pleasant Hill upon the margin of a field over
which the attacking force must advance, with a wooded ravine on
his right forming with his main line of battle an obtuse angle of,
probably, one hundred degrees, and running almost parallel with
the road along which the Confederates were advancing.

The Federal center rested on the edge of the village and found
excellent cover in the numerous ravines into which the friable soil
is here washed by the rains, while the left extended beyond the village and rested upon a dense oak and pine forest.[32]

29. Two standard histories of the campaign list 12,000 Federals and 8,800
Confederates actually engaged at Mansfield. See Johnson, *Red River Campaign*,
140–41; Joiner, *One Damn Blunder*, 103.

30. Churchill was the Confederate officer who had surrendered Arkansas
Post in early 1863. George W. Baylor, an uncle of Walker's wife, had fought on
the Indian frontier in Texas before the war and had been an aide-de-camp to
General Albert Sidney Johnston at Shiloh. He commanded a Texas cavalry regi-
ment during the Red River campaign. See Thomas W. Cutrer, "Baylor, George
Wythe," in Tyler et al., eds., *New Handbook of Texas* 1: 422–23.

31. Pleasant Hill is twenty-one miles southeast of Mansfield and sixteen
miles southwest of Blair's Landing.

32. Students of the battle have been critical of the deployment of Federal

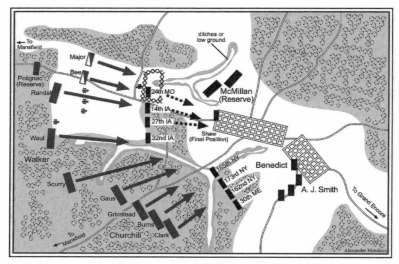

Battle of Pleasant Hill, April 9, 1864

Although Gen. Green had been brought to a halt in his pursuit, Gen. Taylor was firmly convinced that Banks had continued his retreat and that this was but an inconsiderable rear guard of cavalry covering the retreat of the main army. He accordingly ordered Green to charge the enemy, take the position and continue the pursuit. Green attempted to carry out his instructions, the result of which was that in an instant his whole cavalry force was exposed to the fire of the whole Federal right wing, lying, as it were, in ambuscade along the ravine already mentioned and in the pine woods in front. Of course he was driven back, and with heavy loss. Amongst the mortally wounded in this blundering charge was Col. [Augustus C.] Bushell [Buchel], a Prussian officer of great merit.[33]

---

forces at Pleasant Hill, mainly because so many units of Banks's army were scattered and not within supporting distance of each other. See, for example, Johnson, *Red River Campaign*, 166–67.

33. Augustus Buchel, born in Hesse in 1813, had been educated at the finest French and German military academies, served in the French Foreign Legion (where he earned a knighthood for bravery), immigrated to Texas in 1845, and acted as aide-de-camp to Zachary Taylor during the war with Mexico. See Robert W. Stephens, "Buchel, Augustus Carl," in Tyler et al., eds., *New Hand-*

This should have convinced Gen. Taylor of his error, or, at least, have demonstrated the necessity of ascertaining the enemy's position and strength before attempting a further advance. Rendered incautious, however, by the brilliant results of the audacity of yesterday, the Confederate leader was determined to strike a blow before the darkness should afford the enemy further opportunity to escape.[34]

The afternoon was now well advanced, Churchill had been dispatched by an obscure path through the woods to fall upon the enemy's left, beyond and to the south of the village, while Gen. Walker was ordered to form a line of battle to the right of and at right angles with the road from Mansfield, by which we had pursued the enemy, and as soon as Churchill's guns were heard to attack the enemy in front. Hour after hour passed without hearing Churchill's attack, and it was now half past five when his guns were first heard and Walker advanced to the charge. Emerging from the forest through which it was marching "by the right of companies," the line of battle was instantly formed in the open ground and under fire, the brigades of Randal and [Thomas N.] Waul advanced at a run upon the enemy's position,[35] while Scurry was sent more to the right to fill the wide interval left in the direction of Churchill's attack, and to support that officer who had been forced back by overwhelming odds. Scurry in some measure restored affairs in that direction but was eventually forced back with heavy loss, and the whole Confederate right was driven back in confusion. In the meantime the advance of Waul and Randal

---

book of Texas 1: 799–800; Stanley S. McGowen, *Horse Sweat and Powder Smoke: The First Texas Cavalry in the Civil War* (College Station: Texas A&M University Press, 1999).

34. In his history of the war in the Trans-Mississippi, Walker had also criticized Taylor's attitude about the danger of gunboats to infantry and Taylor's placement of the defenses at Fort DeRussy. Although the two men worked closely together in 1863–64 and certainly respected each other, Walker did sometimes disagree with his superior officer's tactics.

35. Brigadier General Thomas N. Waul, a South Carolina native, was a cotton planter in south-central Texas before the war. He had been a strong secessionist in 1861 and a member of the Confederate Congress. He raised his own Texas legion, fought at Vicksburg, and assumed command of James M. Hawes's brigade in February 1864. See Warner, *Generals in Gray,* 328–29.

was fiercely contested, and it was not until the enemy was dislodged from the wooded ravine by a brigade of dismounted cavalry under Col. Baylor that the Federals yielded an inch.[36]

At this juncture Polignac's division, which had been held in reserve, was ordered forward and the whole Confederate left advanced upon the enemy, driving him back with heavy loss upon his center and left with such rapidity that the attention of the enemy on the right was withdrawn from Churchill and Scurry and those officers had opportunity to withdraw from the unequal contest. Night again put an end to the conflict, and although the victory could not be claimed as complete by the Confederates, the result was the utter demoralization and retreat of the Federal army. While the Confederate cavalry occupied the battle field, the infantry was ordered some miles to the rear to the first point where water could be obtained.

The loss on the part of the Federals in killed and wounded was much greater than that of the Confederates, which amounted in killed and wounded and missing to fifteen hundred. But few prisoners were taken on either side.[37]

During the night Banks' whole army retreated, and at dawn the cavalry of Green took up the pursuit, capturing many prisoners and pursuing the retreating army until it found shelter under the guns of Admiral Porter's fleet at Grand Ecore, four miles beyond Nachitoches.[38]

36. Although Walker did not mention it in his history, he was wounded near the road to Mansfield. While riding back and forth along his lines to direct his men, a minie ball or shrapnel (probably mostly spent) struck him in the groin. He remained upright in his saddle for a while, but the pain and shock of the impact took their toll, and he began to lose consciousness. General Taylor rode up and ordered him to be taken to the rear, which Walker feebly protested. He did not return to the head of his columns until the Battle of Jenkins' Ferry, three weeks later, still visibly weak. See Joseph Palmer Blessington, *The Campaigns of Walker's Texas Division* (1875; rpt. Austin, Texas: State House Press, 1994), 73, 197; Taylor, *Destruction and Reconstruction,* 169.

37. The numbers engaged and casualties on both sides were similar: about 12,000 engaged and about 1,500 casualties. See Johnson, *Red River Campaign,* 168–69; Joiner, *One Damn Blunder,* 116.

38. Grand Ecore was a small settlement on a bluff overlooking the Red River, five miles north of Natchitoches.

Banks' army was no longer capable of offensive operations, and such was the demoralization which the battles of Mansfield and Pleasant Hill produced in his still vastly superior army, that not content with the protection of the fleet, a system of elaborate field defenses were thrown up by the incessant labor of his army to protect it against the Confederates, who, relatively, were but a handful. Doubtless it was to have been expected that the whole Confederate force would have thrown itself upon the track of his flying army, but unfortunately for the Confederates, Gen. E. K. Smith was not the leader to comprehend the true line of action, and hesitating several days as if to see if Banks would not again assume the offensive, against the opinion and advice of all his principal subordinates, he unwisely determined to leave the pursuit of Banks to Gen. Taylor, with Polignac's small division of infantry and Green's cavalry,[39] and to dispatch Walker's division and the Missouri division of [Mosby M.] Parsons, and the Arkansas division of Churchill against the Federal army still at Camden under Steele.[40]

To this fatal blunder Banks was indebted for his safety, for it is clearly certain that if the whole force of the Confederates had been thrown upon his shattered and demoralized army its escape, as an organized force, would have been almost impossible.[41] The

39. Although Walker had occasional doubts about some of Taylor's military decisions, the two generals were as one in their low opinion of Kirby Smith, especially his resolve to use most of the army to pursue the Federals on "a wild-goose chase" in Arkansas rather than hound Banks's defeated and demoralized army down the Red River. See Taylor, *Destruction and Reconstruction,* 176, 179 (quotation), 189; Prushankin, *Crisis in Confederate Command.*

40. Brigadier General Parsons, a prominent Democratic politician in Missouri before the war, had fought in the war with Mexico, at Pea Ridge, and at Little Rock. He commanded a small division of Missouri troops in the pursuit of Steele's Federal army in Arkansas. See Warner, *Generals in Gray,* 228–29.

41. Walker and Taylor agreed completely that the Texas division should have joined Taylor in the pursuit of Banks. In messages to Kirby Smith's adjutant, Taylor complained on April 25 that "My plans for following and driving the enemy were to a great extent based upon the assurance that Walker's division would be at my disposal." On May 14: "His [Walker's] presence here at the right time would have insured the most brilliant results." On May 18: "Nothing but the withdrawal of Walker's division from me has prevented the capture of Banks' army and the destruction of Porter's fleet." See *Official Records* 34, pt. 1: 582, 592, 594.

imminence of this danger was heightened by the rapid fall of the waters of Red River, and the consequent necessity of saving the Federal fleet by a timely retreat before the receding water should leave it upon the sands. Already it was doubtful if it could pass the sands at Alexandria, and after a stay of five or six days at Grand Ecore, the further retreat of the Federal army was resumed. This movement was signalized by an unjustifiable act of barbarity in the entire destruction by fire of the town of Compte [Campti], situated on the left bank of the Red River, and a few miles above Grand Ecore. It was known that General Franklin of all the Federal commanders was alone opposed to the indiscriminate pillage and burning that now disgraced the Federal retreat, and that Gen. A. J. Smith, above all others, signalised himself in the completeness with which he carried out the infamous policy now adopted by the discomfited Federal Commander in chief [Lincoln]. Nothing was spared from Grand Ecore to Alexandria, and clouds of smoke by day and pillars of fire by night marked the progress of the retreating army.[42]

It should have been mentioned that a few days after the battle of Pleasant Hill, Gen. Green had been killed in an unwise attack upon a Federal gun boat a few miles above Grand Ecore. The command of the Confederate cavalry now devolved upon Major Gen. [John A.] Wharton, who had recently been detached from the army of Tennessee.[43]

42. Like Walker, Taylor was disgusted with the behavior of Federal troops on their retreat. Taylor blamed A. J. Smith and Smith's association with General William T. Sherman. "It could hardly be expected that troops trained by this commander [Sherman] would respect *the humanities*" (Taylor, *Destruction and Reconstruction,* 193, 195). A member of the 114th New York Infantry agreed: "The wanton and useless destruction of property has well earned [A. J. Smith's] command a lasting disgrace" (Elias P. Pellet, *History of the 114th Regiment, New York State Volunteers* [Norwich, N.Y.: Telegraph and Chronicle Press, 1866], 229).

43. Wharton seemed a worthy successor to the popular Green. A Tennessee-born attorney and large plantation owner in Brazoria County, Texas, before the war, Wharton had been a member of the secession convention and had fought in several major campaigns under Nathan Bedford Forrest and Joseph Wheeler. See Warner, *Generals in Gray,* 331–32; Robert Maberry Jr., "Wharton, John Austin," in Tyler et al., eds., *New Handbook of Texas* 6: 907–8.

꧁꧂

At the close of these operations General Taylor addressed his victorious troops as follows:

> Headquarters—District of West La.
> Mansfield, April 11th, 1864.
> General Orders.
> No.—
> Soldiers of the Army of Western Louisiana:
> At last have your patience and your devotion been rewarded! Condemned for many days to retreat before an overwhelming force, as soon as your reinforcements reached you[,] you turned upon the foe. No language but that of simple narrative should recount your deeds. On the 8th of April you fought the battle of Mansfield. Never in war was a more complete victory won. Attacking the enemy with the utmost alacrity when the order was given the result was not for a moment doubtful. The enemy was driven from every position, his artillery captured, his men routed. In vain new, fresh troops were brought up. Your magnificent line, like a resistless wave, swept everything before it. Night alone stopped your advance. Twenty one pieces of artillery, twenty five hundred prisoners, many stands of colors, two hundred and fifty wagons attest your success over the 13th and 19th Army Corps. On the 9th you took up the pursuit and pressed it with vigor. For twelve miles prisoners, scattered arms, burning wagons proved how well the previous day's work had been done by the soldiers of Texas and Louisiana. The gallant divisions from Missouri and Arkansas, unfortunately absent on the 8th, marched forty five miles in two days to share the glories of Pleasant Hill. This was emphatically the soldier's victory.[44] In spite of the strength of the enemy's position, held by fresh troops of the 16th Corps, your valor and devotion triumphed over all. Darkness closed one of the hottest fights of the war. The morning of the 10th dawned upon a flying foe, with our cavalry in pursuit, capturing prisoners at every step. But these glorious victories were dearly won. A list

---

44. Although the battle at Pleasant Hill was a tactical standoff, Taylor considered it a strategic victory because the Federal army abandoned the drive toward Shreveport and retreated in some disorder down the Red River.

of the heroic dead would sadden the sternest heart. A visit to the hospitals would move the sympathy of the most unfeeling. The memory of our dead will live as long as noble deeds are cherished on earth. The consciousness of duty well performed will alleviate the suffering of the wounded. Soldiers! From a thousand homes thanks will ascend to the God of battles for your victories. Tender wives and fond mothers will repose in safety behind the breastwork of your valor. No fears will be felt that the hated foe will desecrate their homes by his presence. This is your reward, but much remains to be done. Strict discipline, prompt obedience to orders, cheerful endurance of privations will alone assure our independence.

R. Taylor
Major General Comdg.

CHAPTER 4.

The Arkansas Campaign and the Battle of the Saline

Leaving Gen. Banks to pursue his retreat, followed by the diminished forces of Gen. Taylor, let us turn our attention in another direction. Gen. Steele was still at Camden, in ignorance of the defeat of Banks, but such was the condition of the roads and the failing strength of his draft animals upon which he depended to bring his subsistence from the Arkansas River, that he found it impossible to advance upon Shreveport in accordance with the plan of campaign agreed upon with Banks. He therefore seems to have contemplated the permanent occupation of the Ouachita valley, and wait for a better condition of roads before attempting a further advance southwards.

On the 15th and 16th of April the infantry divisions of Walker, Parsons, and Churchill passed through Shreveport, crossed Red River upon a pontoon bridge, and took up their line of march for Camden. In the meantime Steele's position was growing critical by the failing of his animals. The superior force of Price prevented his drawing supplies from the surrounding country, and the greater portion of his cavalry were already dismounted by the dearth and extreme poverty of their horses. Finally he determined to make an effort to procure forage, and dispatched a train of several hundred wagons to the comparatively fertile country lying to the westward, under the escort of a brigade of infantry, one regiment of which being negroes. At a place called Poison Spring, sixteen miles west of Camden, they were attacked by Gen. [Samuel Bell] Maxey,[1] in command of Gano's Brigade, the friendly Cherokees, and Marma-

---

1. A Kentucky native, graduate of the famed West Point Class of 1846, and decorated veteran of the war with Mexico, Maxey raised a Texas infantry regiment early in the war and served as a brigadier general in the Western Theater before being transferred to the Trans-Mississippi Department in late 1863. See Louise Horton, "Maxey, Samuel Bell," in Tyler et al., eds., *New Handbook of Texas* 4: 580–81; Warner, *Generals in Gray*, 216.

duke's Missouri cavalry, and the whole force was destroyed, or captured.[2]

Gen. E. K. Smith, who had now taken the field in person, was yet in doubt as to the intentions of Gen. Banks. Taylor's reduced forces were numerically inferior to the enemy as three to one, and had the Federal commander had the courage to resume the offensive, he could still have forced his way by the weight of numbers, to Shreveport. Finally the information that Banks had recommenced his retreat from Grand Ecore determined the Confederate commander [Smith] to turn his serious attention to Gen. Steele, with the hope of entirely destroying or capturing his army.[3]

On the afternoon of the 26th of April the entire Confederate force reached the neighborhood of Camden to learn that the Federal force had evacuated Camden, crossed the Ouachita River, and taken the road [north] towards Little Rock. Of course Steele had taken the precaution to destroy all means of crossing the river, and in consequence of the failure of the [Confederate] pontoon train to come up, it was not until the afternoon of the next day that the engineer troops under Captain Buhlow had constructed a temporary foot bridge, and raised and bailed out a single ferry flat, the complete destruction of which had been overlooked by the retiring Federals. By means of the bridge and boat the infantry of Price and Walker, with four light batteries and an ambulance to each regiment had been crossed and took up the pursuit of the enemy.

In the meantime, before the arrival of the infantry at Camden, Gen. Price had dispatched Gen. Fagan with three hundred horsemen to the rear of Steele in order to intercept a large supply train

2. At Poison Spring, about twelve miles northwest of Camden, Confederate cavalry captured all two hundred supply wagons and routed the Federal escorting force on April 18. Some Federals charged that Confederates had killed wounded enemy soldiers and some who tried to surrender, especially African Americans. Contrary to Walker's account, about 800 of the 1,100 Federals survived and eventually returned to Camden. Nevertheless, the desperately needed corn they had gathered was lost. See Edwin C. Bearss, *Steele's Retreat from Camden and the Battle of Jenkins' Ferry* (Little Rock: Arkansas Civil War Centennial Commission, 1967), 15–41; Anne J. Bailey, "Was There a Massacre at Poison Spring?" *Military History of the Southwest* 20 (Fall 1990): 157–68.

3. *Official Records* 34, pt. 1: 481, 534, 555, 582; pt. 3: 786. Lowe, *Walker's Texas Division*, 215.

known to be on the road from Pine Bluff, on the Saline river, which was escorted by two regiments of Ohio volunteers and a light battery. The Federals were surprised, and both men and material consisting of thirteen hundred prisoners, six pieces of artillery, and six hundred wagons laden with subsistence, fell into the hands of the Confederates.[4]

Orders were now dispatched to Gen. Fagan to send his prisoners and booty across the Ouachita, and with the remainder of his force to throw himself in front of Steele, and by obstructing the roads, and in every other way possible, delay Steele's retreating column until the infantry now on his track could overtake him. It is to the failure of this officer to receive these instructions, and to his want of enterprise in the absence of instructions to pursue a source dictated by every instinct of a soldier, that Steele owes the escape of his army from utter destruction. Marmaduke had also been ordered to throw himself in front of the Federal column, but he was not able to make the immense circuit necessary to succeed, and was only able to overtake Steele's rear guard on the afternoon of the 29th.

Walker's and Price's infantry was now within hearing of Steele's and Marmaduke's guns, and after a few hours of repose, took up the pursuit at one o'clock in the morning in a drenching rain which continued to fall during the greater part of the following day. In the meantime Steele's column had reached the Saline river, a stream now swollen to a level with its banks by the heavy rains still falling. Across it he had thrown a pontoon bridge, upon which he might have crossed over his infantry and artillery during the night by the sacrifice of his baggage and commissariat trains. To save these was the object of the battle [Jenkins' Ferry] that followed. On the part of the Confederate commander he was now well

4. Again, Walker was generally correct about the April 25 Battle of Marks' Mills (about forty miles northeast of Camden), but his account was based on overly optimistic Confederate reports. The Federal train included about 300 wagons, not 600; the wagons were mostly empty, not laden with supplies; and the Confederates numbered about 2,500, not 300. The loss of this second entire train and 1,300 more men convinced General Steele the time had come for a hasty retreat to Little Rock (Sutherland, "1864," 117–19; Bearss, *Steele's Retreat,* 42–86).

assured that Steele would escape across the swollen waters of the Saline, unless he crushed him here. Consequently he determined to bring on a general engagement. For fear that Steele would endeavor to escape before a reconnaissance of the position could be made, Price, whose division was in the lead, was hurried to the attack of the Federals, posted most advantageously, although his [Price's} brigades struggling through the mud and rain arrived exhausted upon the field.

Three miles before reaching the Saline the road descends from the piney hills into the alluvial bottom of the river. The heavy rains of the last few days had rendered this road, after the passage of a few of the leading vehicles of Steele's army, almost impassable, and his wagons drawn by his lean and weak animals were utterly unable to drag their loads after them. Heavy details of men were made to assist the exhausted animals, and, this tedious process of drawing wagons one by one through the mud to a place of safety beyond the river gave the Confederates time to come up.

But Steele occupied a position that could not well have been more favorable. Immediately on the left of the road where it descends to the lowlands was a small stream, now deep and rapid,

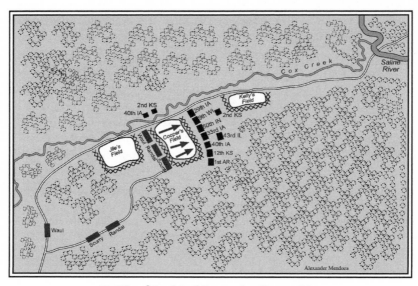

Battle of Jenkins' Ferry, April 30, 1864

which rested on his right, while his left was protected by lowlands now under water from six [inches] to two feet in depth. The intermediate space was occupied by a large cotton field. Beyond this in the edge of the woods with the open ground in his front, Steele had posted his infantry, who were further sheltered by temporary breast works of rails. Here the same fatal blunder was committed as at Pleasant Hill, and the enemy was attacked before any information was gained as to his position or the nature of the ground. Marmaduke, who had been skirmishing with the enemy since dawn, received his first supports from the infantry of Price at 6 o'clock in the morning, and brigade after brigade of Churchill's and Parson's divisions were pushed to his support as they struggled up to the front through the mud and rain. No wonder that the attack was feeble and easily repulsed. In the meantime Walker's division of Texans were coming up as rapidly as possible. By this time some slight knowledge of the field had been gained by Gen. E. K. Smith, and orders were sent by him to Gen. Walker to send one of his brigades direct to the front where Price was now engaged, and with the other two to make a detour to the right, and, if possible, turn the left of the enemy and attack him in the rear. It was found impracticable to gain the rear of the enemy's position for the reasons already mentioned [i.e., the flooded river bottom], and as the battle was still raging on the left, this officer [Walker] formed his line of battle [on the] nearest firm ground to the enemy's left flank, and, with the front well covered by skirmishers, the division, by the right of companies, advanced through the wooded swamp until the enemy's skirmishers were reached, when the complete deployment of the line was instantly effected, and the Texans, with a shout, advanced upon the enemy who, on their part, were making a flank movement to envelop Price who was still feebly contending on the Federal right.

Up to this time the brigade of Waul, of Walker's division, which had advanced by the direct road, had been held in reserve, but was now pushed to the front by Gen. Smith across the field already mentioned, but was unable to force the enemy from their rail breastworks. In the meantime Price's troops were withdrawn to the rear, reformed, and reported to Gen. Walker on the right, who was now driving the enemy back with heavy loss. Already he had lost his three brigade commanders, two of them mortally wounded, and it was doubtful if he could long continue the contest as he was touching upon his last cartridge.[5] At this juncture Gen. Parsons' Missouri division came to his support, which by wading waist deep through the wooded bog gained a position on the right [Walker's right, the Federal left] and rear of the enemy's line of battle, and forced him to fall back along his whole line and ultimately to retreat across the pontoon bridge, which he destroyed behind him, leaving a large number of wagons hopelessly bogged behind.[6]

The exhaustion of the Confederates was so complete that after the retreat of the enemy the men threw themselves down for repose in the mud and water where they stood. With no other subsistence than that contained in their haversacks, and no commissariat wagons in attendance, they had marched three days and nights almost continuously, broken only by a few hours for daily repose. The hope of capturing or destroying Steele's whole army, however, buoyed up those devoted men, but now that the excitement was ended they sank down in utter fatigue.

The Confederate loss was very heavy, amounting in killed and wounded to more than nine hundred. That of the Federals was less, probably not exceeding six hundred. Amongst the wounded, on the Confederate side, were Brig. Generals Scurry, Randal, and Waul, of Walker's division, the first two mortally.[7]

5. All three brigade commanders in Walker's division fell within a single hour. General Waul was shot through the arm, which broke the bone and caused heavy bleeding. He never commanded his brigade again after Jenkins' Ferry. Horace Randal was shot through the abdomen and died two days later. A Federal bullet pierced General Scurry's side and exited his body on the opposite side. He remained conscious on the field for the rest of the fight, but a wound to the body cavity was usually fatal, and he died the next day. After the war the state of Texas named two counties for Randal and Scurry (Lowe, *Walker's Texas Division*, 225–26).

6. Although General Parsons and his lieutenants believed their assault on the Federal left had initiated the Union withdrawal from the field, later historians generally conclude that the decision to abandon the fight had already been made. The timing of Parsons's advance and the general retreat of the Federals convinced Walker that the Missouri division had guaranteed the victory. See *Official Records* 34, pt. 1: 810, 814–15; Bearss, *Steele's Retreat*, 156–59.

7. For casualties at Jenkins' Ferry, see *Official Records* 34, pt. 1: 557, 692, 758.

The capture of Steele's supply at Marks' Mills, and the destitution of the country which afforded nothing for the subsistence of an army, even if no enemy had been pursuing, were circumstances causing the Federal commander the utmost embarrassment. Even the half and quarter rations he had been issuing to his troops since leaving Camden would soon be exhausted, and he had no hopes of subsistence short of Little Rock. Added to this the failing strength of his starved and exhausted animals compelled him to sacrifice the greater portion of his baggage and commissariat wagons, even those he had succeeded in placing beyond the Saline, and his army henceforward was broken up into a straggling mass of men seeking food, which was yet forty five miles distant.

There is little doubt, therefore, that could the cavalry of Marmaduke and Fagan, the latter especially, have come up at the close of the action, and crossed the Saline, the greater portion of Steele's army would have been captured or destroyed. As an evidence of this it may be mentioned that a Texas Lieutenant [Colonel], who happened to be on the north side of the Saline, with eight hundred men, followed up the retreating Federals, and captured and brought in forty eight prisoners with their arms.[8] In this sad plight, in squads of stragglers, Steele's army reached Little Rock.[9]

The result of the operations that have been described in the foregoing pages had been most disastrous to the Federal arms. Banks[,] defeated with heavy loss in two pitched battles[,] had been driven back to Alexandria, and now Steele who was to have cooperated in the conquest of the Trans-Mississippi States, after heavy sacrifices, had barely saved his army by a disastrous re-

---

Estimates by historians generally agree with Walker: of 6,000 Confederates engaged, 900-plus casualties; of 4,000 Federals, 700-plus. See Bearss, *Steele's Retreat,* 161; Johnson, *Red River Campaign,* 202; Joiner, *One Damn Blunder,* 134; Sutherland, "1864," 123.

8. Lieutenant Colonel Benjamin Elliott's 1st Missouri Cavalry Battalion pursued Steele's retreating army for three days, to within twenty miles of Little Rock, and forced the Federals to burn 220 more wagons and great piles of supplies to prevent their capture. See *Official Records* 34, pt. 1: 840.

9. When Steele's bedraggled army limped back into Little Rock on May 3, it was lighter by 2,750 soldiers, six cannons, 635 wagons, and 2,500 mules than when it set out on its adventure toward the Red River six weeks earlier. See Johnson, *Red River Campaign,* 203–4.

treat. The former might still entertain the idea of strengthening himself at Alexandria, hold the lower valley of Red River, and still threaten the upper valley of that river and seek to penetrate into eastern and middle Texas, regions of great fertility, and upon which the entire Confederate army west of the Mississippi depended in a great measure for subsistence. Besides, the loss of the immense grazing grounds of that State would be a severe blow to the Cis-Mississippi army, which notwithstanding the loss of Vicksburg and the partial blockade of this great highway by the fleets of the enemy, still continued to supply vast numbers of the finest beef cattle for its consumption, and the loss of those supplies might have been disastrous.[10]

The temptation to follow Steele and force him to evacuate the whole State of Arkansas was certainly most inviting. The consideration above stated, however, added to the immense difficulty of bringing supplies from Red River, and the lower Ouachita, in the then condition of the roads was so enormous as to be practically impossible. Hence the further pursuit of Steele was reluctantly abandoned, and, after a rest a [*sic*] two or three days, near the battle field, the burial of the dead of the two armies, and the establishment of temporary hospitals for the wounded friends and enemies, the infantry returned to Camden, and in a few days thereafter took up its line of march for the lower Red River to reinforce Gen. Taylor.[11]

10. Thousands of Trans-Mississippi beef cattle were swum across the Mississippi River to Confederate armies east of the river after the fall of Vicksburg and Port Hudson, even as late as the winter of 1864–65. See *Official Records* 46, pt. 2: 1222; Frank E. Vandiver, "Texas and the Confederate Army's Meat Problem," *Southwestern Historical Quarterly* 47 (January 1944): 225–33.

11. During the forced march to reinforce Taylor, General Walker replaced his fallen brigadiers. Richard Waterhouse took command of Scurry's brigade. A Tennessee native, he had been a merchant in East Texas before the war and raised the Nineteenth Texas Infantry from the area around Jefferson, Texas. Robert P. Maclay, a Pennsylvania native and member of the West Point Class of 1840, had been serving as Walker's chief of staff before taking command of Randal's brigade. Wilburn King, a Georgia native who had commanded the Eighteenth Texas Infantry, replaced General Waul, still convalescing in Texas. See Thomas W. Cutrer, "Waterhouse, Richard," in Tyler et al., eds., *New Handbook of Texas* 6: 841. For Maclay, see Arthur W. Bergeron Jr., "Robert Plunket Maclay," in William C. Davis, ed., *The Confederate General*, 6 vols. (Harrisburg,

It may be mentioned as evidence opposed to the received Northern opinion that Southern troops are wanting in physical stamina and powers of endurance, that the infantry division of Gen. Walker, composed entirely of Texans, from the 13th. of March to the 30th. of April, or forty eight days, marched six hundred and twenty eight miles and fought three pitched battles, and after a repose of five days only set out for the lower Red River valley, a distance of one hundred and ninety miles, which it accomplished in eight days.[12]

Pa.: National Historical Society, 1991), vol. 6: 190–91. For King, see Arthur W. Bergeron Jr., "Wilburn Hill King," *New Handbook of Texas* 6: 186–87; Wilburn Hill King, *With the 18th Texas Infantry: The Autobiography of Wilburn Hill King,* ed. L. David Norris (Hillsboro, Texas: Hill College Press, 1996).

12. Walker's pride in his division might have been even greater if he had had the advantage of modern maps and mileage charts. In fact, his men marched at least as far as he estimated (818 miles) and probably farther (850 miles) from mid-March to early May. The latter number represents the approximate straight-line distance from Washington, D.C., to Memphis, Tennessee. To place this feat in context, compare Sherman's March of 285 miles in five weeks to Walker's march (with three major battles) of 630 miles in seven weeks. See Lowe, *Walker's Texas Division,* 228.

CHAPTER 5.

The Federal Evacuation of Red River Valley

We left General Taylor in pursuit of Banks' flying and demoralized army, and we will now resume the narrative of the events that resulted in its expulsion from the valley of the Red River. With so considerable an army at his disposal, still numbering quite thirty thousand men, with a numerous and formidable fleet of war vessels, and another of transports, that Gen. Banks no longer dreamed of invasion and occupation but of safety, demonstrated the extent to which demoralization and panic existed in his army. Twice defeated on consecutive days was a misfortune calculated to shake the sturdiness even of veterans, but the effect was heightened immensely by the feeling that their General was utterly incapable of extricating them from the dangers which his blundering had created.[1] His attempt to cast the responsibility of his defeat upon his Chief of Staff, Gen. [Charles P.] Stone, whom he sent in arrest to New Orleans, only deepened their distrust and aversion.[2] No matter what may have been the causes which produced it, that great demoralization did exist must be admitted, otherwise the almost sauve qui peut flight of Gen. Banks' army before a handful of pursuing Confederates cannot otherwise be accounted for. The latter consisted of one infantry division of two brigades, numbering, since the losses of the 8th and 9th, scarcely two thousand men, and of Gen. Wharton's cavalry corps of four brigades, or about four thousand five hundred men, and about forty eight pieces of field artillery. This does not include a brigade of cavalry, with two

1. Johnson, *Red River Campaign,* 206, 216, describes the soldiers' bitter reaction to Banks.

2. Walker, like many observers then and since, believed Banks used Stone as a scapegoat for his (Banks's) own failings during the campaign. See Johnson, *Red River Campaign,* 217–18; James M. McPherson, *Battle Cry of Freedom: The Civil War Era* (New York: Oxford University Press, 1988), 362–63.

field batteries, operating on the north or left bank of Red River, under Brig. Gen. Liddell.[3]

Penetrating the purpose of the Federal General to withdraw from his cooped up position at Grand Ecore, Gen. Taylor dispatched Brig. Gen. [Hamilton P.] Bee with a portion of Wharton's cavalry and some light batteries to take up a position at Monette's Ferry, on Cane River, a branch of Red River, forty five miles [by river] below Nachitoches, and to dispute the crossing of the Federal army.[4]

Making a détour through the pine forest to the south of Cane River Gen. Bee occupied, on the morning of the 21st of April, a most advantageous position upon the wooded bluffs overlooking the open and level plain along which the Federal army was advancing. Gen. Bee's force was entirely insufficient to bar the passage of a retreating army, but the position itself was so advantageous that with a more skilful handling of his troops, and a more vigorous resistance, the Federal army would have found it extremely difficult to dislodge their enemy and to force a passage.[5]

Cane River which branching off from Red River at Grand Ecore, and skirting for more than forty five miles a succession of pine clad hills, reenters the parent stream eight miles below the main road to Alexandria, which crosses the Cane River at Monette's Ferry. The island thus formed is of extremely [rich] fertility, and in a

3. St. John R. Liddell, a forty-eight-year-old Louisiana planter, had fought in the Western Theater before being transferred to the Trans-Mississippi Department. With fewer than six hundred men and only one four-gun battery (and that only briefly), he harassed Porter's gunboats from the left bank of the Red River but could not halt the Federal retreat. See *Official Records* 34, pt. 1: 633–37; Warner, *Generals in Gray*, 187–88.

4. Hamilton P. Bee had moved to Texas from South Carolina with his family when he was a boy. He had served as a Texas Ranger during the Mexican War and as a state representative in Texas in the 1840s. Appointed a brigadier general in early 1862, he had little military experience by the time he led troops in the pursuit of Banks's army. See Thomas W. Cutrer, "Bee, Hamilton Prioleau," in Tyler et al., eds., *New Handbook of Texas* 1: 458; Warner, *Generals in Gray*, 24–25.

5. Walker's assessment of Bee's position and performance has been echoed in many later historical accounts of the campaign. For examples, see Johnson, *Red River Campaign*, 233–34; Joiner, *One Damn Blunder*, 153–57.

high state of cultivation. For several hours the march of the Federal army towards Bee's position could be distinctly seen by this handful of Confederates, however, whose presence was entirely unsuspected. Finally this moving mass came within range of the Confederate batteries, which, very unskillfully, opened upon the enemy's column en route, at a very long range, which had no other effect than to produce the utmost consternation. The 13th and 19th Army Corps were at once deployed, and several hours passed in preparations to force a passage over Cane River, which was finally forded by a column of infantry several thousand strong, and, after a feeble resistance from Bee's dismounted cavalry, the heights were carried, and the passage of the river secured.[6]

While this was taking place Gen. Wharton, with the remainder of his cavalry and Polignac's division, was following up the retreating army. The rear guard composed of the 16th and part of the 17th Army Corps under Major Gen. A. J. Smith was overtaken at Clutesville [Cloutierville], and while Bee's batteries were thundering in advance, Wharton's were heard attacking the rear. Wharton, as Bee had been, was too weak to effect anything decisive, and after a sharp engagement of some hours the Federal army was permitted to pursue its retreat unmolested.

The conduct of the Federal army on this retreat will be a standing disgrace to the Federal arms for all time, as many generations must pass away before the devastation and wanton destruction of towns, villages, and farm houses will be forgotten or forgiven. The perpetrators of these acts of barbarism were worse enemies of the cause of the Union than the so called "rebels" in arms, and to the minds of the sufferers, and their descendants, this cause will forever be represented by the ashes and blackened ruins of their once peaceful and happy homes, and the names of Banks and A. J. Smith will be uttered with the execrations of a ruined people for generations to come.[7]

6. Years later, Taylor still regretted Bee's disappointing performance at Monett's Ferry: "General Bee had exhibited much personal gallantry in the charge at Pleasant Hill, but he was without experience in war, and had neglected to study the ground or strengthen his position at Monette's" (Taylor, *Destruction and Reconstruction,* 182).

7. Walker was generally respectful, sometimes even admiring, in his obser-

As in the ascent of Red River, the Federal fleet attempted to descend no faster than the daily marches of the army, to afford a point d'appui in case of an attack by the Confederates in force. The rapid falling of the water, however, now threatened him with a more imminent danger, and forced him to proceed with all dispatch to Alexandria. In this descent his transports were greatly harrassed by the light batteries of the Confederates, who, having the undisturbed possession of the left bank of the river, could select favorable positions, and when forced from them by the iron clad fleet could take up others further in advance.[8]

This they could now do without difficulty since the low stage of water rendered the descent difficult and dangerous. The Confederates were now much less in awe of Federal gun boats than formerly, and even iron clads were fearlessly attacked whenever encountered. [Timothy D.] Nettles['s], [B. Felix] Winchester's and [George] Ralston's batteries greatly distinguished themselves in these encounters.[9] In one of these the formidable iron clad "Eastport," Admiral Porter's flagship, was grounded, and all attempts to get her afloat proving abortive she was scuttled and abandoned.[10]

---

vations of his old home, the U.S. Army, but he was angry and unforgiving in his comments about the widespread and apparently gratuitous destruction left in the wake of Generals Banks and A. J. Smith. Even some of their fellow officers in Union service were appalled. William Franklin offered a reward of five hundred dollars for information leading to convictions of those who had committed the "indiscriminate marauding and incendiarism, disgraceful to the army of a civilized nation." See *Official Records* 34, pt. 3: 307.

8. The commander of the six hundred Confederates on the left bank, General Liddell, had only one four-gun battery, and even that was not available to him for most of the retreat. Thus, the harassment of Federal gunboats from the left bank came primarily from the muskets and rifles of his dismounted troopers. The main body of Taylor's little army on the right bank used field artillery and small arms to make life miserable for the retreating sailors.

9. Captain Timothy D. Nettles's Twelfth Texas Field Battery (much better known as the Val Verde Battery), Captain B. Felix Winchester's Fifth Louisiana Field Battery (better known as the Pelican Artillery), and Captain George Ralston's Mississippi Battery.

10. Walker was correct about the destruction of the *Eastport*, a gigantic ironclad normally armed with eight heavy naval guns. The tinclad *Black Hawk* traditionally served as Porter's flagship. See Silverstone, *Warships of the Civil War Navies*, 156, 164; Joiner, *One Damn Blunder*, 148. The remains of the river behe-

Several valuable steam transports were captured without being materially damaged, and afterwards proved of great service to the Confederates.

After being thus harrassed, Admiral Porter arrived with his fleet at Alexandria, but found to his great dismay that the depth of water in the river was insufficient to float his most valuable vessels over the falls at that point. Banks' dispirited and disorganized army finally reached the same point, continually harrassed upon the rear and flanks by Wharton's cavalry. Since Gen. Taylor's force was insufficient to justify a general engagement, he showed great activity in the pursuit of the enemy, and added to their demoralization and panic by constant attacks at exposed points and keeping up night and day a state of constant alarm.

Brig. Gen. [James P.] Major, with two brigades of Texas cavalry, now took up a position with three light batteries at old Fort De Russy, below Alexandria, and after capturing and destroying, or forcing their crews to blow up two gun boats and several transports, succeeded in completely blockading Red River, and cutting off Banks' supplies, which could only reach him by river.[11] In this critical situation Banks commenced preparations for the evacuation of Alexandria, and the abandonment of Admiral Porter and his fleet to their fate. Against this Porter remonstrated so strongly, even threatening, it was said, to fire upon Banks' forces should they attempt to cross the pontoon bridge in front of Alexandria,

---

moth were located 130 years later near Montgomery, about fifteen miles southeast of Natchitoches. See Charles E. Pearson et al., *Historical Assessment and Magnetometer and Terrestrial Surveys of the Gunboat U.S.S. Eastport and Steamboat Edward F. Dix, Red River Waterway, Grant Parish, Louisiana, Final Report,* performed for the U.S. Army Corps of Engineers, Vicksburg District, Vicksburg, Miss. (Baton Rouge, La.: Coastal Environments, Inc., 1995).

11. Major's ambushes and volleys from the right bank of the Red River on May 4–5 inflicted a stinging reverse on the U.S. Navy, which lost two gunboats, three transports, and six hundred sailors killed and wounded. To compound the Federals' misery, the Confederates closed the Red River to Union shipping for days. See Johnson, *Red River Campaign,* 255–57; Navy Department, *Official Records of the Union and Confederate Navies in the War of the Rebellion,* 31 vols. (Washington: Government Printing Office, 1894–1922), ser. 1, vol. 26: 113–28, 134.

that flight of the Federal army was for the time stayed,[12] while under the orders of the engineers a force was got to work to construct a dam below the Falls, and so near as to deepen the water sufficiently to permit the fleet to pass below.[13]

In this work, the [Federal] army, or as many as could be profitably employed, spent the latter part of April, and succeeded in saving the fleet which passed in safety to the deep water below the falls [on May 9–13].

In the meantime the blockade of Red River had produced scarcity in the Federal camp, and the expedition for the conquest of Louisiana and Texas having already proved abortive, Banks determined to place his shattered and discontented army in a place of safety. This was growing more and more imperative since the defeat of Steele in Arkansas had freed the Confederate army in that State, which was marching to reinforce Gen. Taylor. On the 12th of May Gen. Banks commenced his march from Alexandria, the greater portion of which he burned to the ground, and took his line of march for the Mississippi, along the right bank of Red River.

As on his retreat from Grand Ecore, his rear was followed up and harrassed at every step by the Confederates, Brig. Gen. William Steele, with a division of Wharton's cavalry, inflicting a serious loss upon the rear guard, as formerly commanded by A. J. Smith, and consisting of the 16th. Army Corps.[14]

12. Although Banks and Porter clashed on more than one occasion during this campaign, the charge that Banks planned to abandon the riverboats above the falls at Alexandria was unfounded. Porter certainly suspected that Banks might abandon the navy to its fate, but Banks promised to (and did) delay the army's departure from Alexandria in order to protect the riverboats. See Hollandsworth, *Pretense of Glory*, 200, 202; Hearn, *Admiral David Dixon Porter*, 255, 262; Johnson, *Red River Campaign*, 264–65.

13. Federal engineers partially dammed the river in order to raise the water level, thereby permitting Porter's riverboats to scrape through the shallow water to deeper water (and safety) below the dam. See Richard B. Irwin, "The Red River Campaign," in Johnson and Buel, eds., *Battles and Leaders* 4: 358–60; Joiner, *One Damn Blunder*, 159–68; Johnson, *Red River Campaign*, 260–66.

14. William Steele, a New York native who fought for the Confederacy, was a graduate of the U.S. Military Academy (Class of 1840). He had briefly com-

In the meantime Gen. Taylor with Polignac's division and the remainder of Wharton's cavalry, was in advance of Banks, at the crossing of Bayou des Glaises, and the day of the 15th [of May] was spent in harmless artillery practice by the batteries of the two forces, until the coming up of A. J. Smith enabled Banks to brush Taylor's small force out of his way and to resume his retreat.[15]

On the next day major Gen. Wharton, being in command of the Confederate [cavalry] forces, the enemy's rear was again attacked at Norwood's Plantation, four miles west of the Atchafalaya, and, owing to a misunderstanding as to the distance Polignac's division was from the field, the attack was premature, and resulted in the disastrous repulse of the Confederates and the loss of several hundred prisoners.[16] The next day Banks' whole army crossed the Atchafalaya at Simmsport, the fleet of Admiral Porter passed out of Red River into the Mississippi, and the invasion of North Western Louisiana was terminated.

---

manded Green's cavalry division before General Wharton assumed control of that unit. See Warner, *Generals in Gray,* 289–90; [no author], "Steele, William," in Tyler et al., eds., *New Handbook of Texas* 6: 79.

15. Walker referred here to the Battle of Mansura, Louisiana, fought on a broad, flat prairie, about eight miles south of Fort De Russy on May 16. Taylor's report of the action is in *Official Records* 34, pt. 1: 592–93.

16. The Battle of Yellow Bayou, fourteen miles southeast of Mansura and about three miles west of Simmesport (where the Red River Campaign had begun two months earlier), was the final Confederate attempt to strike at Banks before he crossed the Atchafalaya and Mississippi rivers to safety. The next day (May 19) the Federals crossed the Atchafalaya River and took their bridge with them, leaving the Confederates in control of the contested ground, central Louisiana and the Red River Valley.

Bibliography

Primary Sources

MANUSCRIPTS

Black, John C., and Family. Papers. Illinois State Historical Library, Springfield.

Membership Applications, 1889–1970. Sons of the American Revolution. Ancestry.com on-line database. Provo, Utah: Ancestry.com Operations, Inc., 2011.

Porter, John C. "Early Days of Pittsburg, Texas, 1859–1874; 18th Texas Infantry, Company H, Life of John C. Porter and Sketch of His Experiences in the Civil War." 18th Texas Infantry file. Historical Research Center, Hill College, Hillsboro, Texas.

Ralston, Joseph Courtney. Reminiscences. Vanderslice-Ralston Family Papers. In possession of Becky Vanderslice, Boulder, Colo.

Walker, John G. "The War of Secession West of the Mississippi River During the Years 1863–4– & 5." Myron Gwinner Collection. U.S. Army Military History Institute, Carlisle Barracks, Pa.

Wallace, Harvey Alexander. Papers. Southwest Arkansas Regional Archives, Washington, Ark.

GOVERNMENT DOCUMENTS

Bureau of the Census. Fifth Census of the United States (Howard County, Missouri), 1830. Records of the Bureau of the Census. Record Group 29. National Archives, Washington, D.C.

————. *Population of the United States in 1860; Compiled from the Original Returns of the Eighth Census.* Compiled by Joseph C. G. Kennedy. Washington, D.C.: Government Printing Office, 1864.

Case Files of Applications from Former Confederates for Presidential Pardons ("Amnesty Papers"), 1865–67. Records of the Adjutant General's Office, 1780s–1917. Record Group 94. National Archives, Washington, D.C.

Compiled Service Records of Confederate General and Staff Officers, and Nonregimental Enlisted Men, 1861–65. War Department Collection of Confederate Records, 1825–1900. Record Group 109. National Archives, Washington, D.C.

Despatches from U.S. Ministers (Colombia). General Records of the Department of State, 1756–1993. Record Group 59. National Archives, Washington, D.C.

Navy Department. *Official Records of the Union and Confederate Navies in the War of the Rebellion.* 31 vols. Washington, D.C.: Government Printing Office, 1894–1922.

Pearson, Charles E., et al. *Historical Assessment and Magnetometer and Terrestrial Surveys of the Gunboat U.S.S. Eastport and Steamboat Edward F. Dix, Red River Waterway, Grant Parish, Louisiana, Final Report.* Performed for the U.S. Army Corps of Engineers, Vicksburg District, Vicksburg, Miss. Baton Rouge, La.: Coastal Environments, Inc., 1995.

Records of Governor Pendleton Murrah, 1863–1865. Archives and Information Services Division, Texas State Library and Archives Commission. Austin.

War Department. *The War of the Rebellion: A Compilation of the Official Records of the Union and Confederate Armies.* 128 vols. Washington, D.C.: Government Printing Office, 1880–1901.

NEWSPAPERS

Charleston (S.C.) *Mercury,* 1864
Washington Post, 1893
Winchester (Va.) *Times,* 1893

BOOKS

Bergeron, Arthur W., Jr., ed. *The Civil War Reminiscences of Major Silas T. Grisamore, C.S.A.* Baton Rouge: Louisiana State University Press, 1993.

Blessington, Joseph Palmer. *The Campaigns of Walker's Texas Division.* 1875. Rpt. with new introductions by Norman D. Brown and T. Michael Parrish. Austin, Texas: State House Press, 1994.

Bliss, Zenas R. *The Reminiscences of Major General Zenas R. Bliss, 1854–1876: From the Texas Frontier to the Civil War and Back Again.* Ed. Thomas T. Smith, Jerry D. Thompson, Robert Wooster, and Ben E. Pingenot. Austin: Texas State Historical Assn., 2007.

Deibert, Ralph C. *A History of the Third United States Cavalry.* Harrisburg, Pa.: Telegraph Press, 1933.

Dorsey, Sarah A. *Recollections of Henry Watkins Allen, Brigadier-General, Confederate States Army, Ex-Governor of Louisiana.* New Orleans: J. A. Gresham, 1866.

Evans, Clement A., ed. *Confederate Military History: A Library of Confederate States History.* 12 vols. Atlanta: Confederate Publishing Co., 1899.

Forrest, Douglas French. *Odyssey in Gray: A Diary of Confederate Service, 1863–1865.* Ed. William N. Still Jr. Richmond: Virginia State Library, 1979.

Johnson, Robert Underwood, and Clarence Clough Buel, eds. *Battles and Leaders of the Civil War.* 4 vols. New York: Century, 1887–88.

King, Wilburn Hill. *With the 18th Texas Infantry: The Autobiography of Wilburn Hill King.* Ed. L. David Norris. Hillsboro, Texas: Hill College Press, 1996.

Niccol, Robert. *Essay on Sugar, and General Treatise on Sugar Refining.* Greenock, Scotland: A. MacKenzie & Co., 1864.

Pellet, Elias P. *History of the 114th Regiment, New York State Volunteers.* Norwich, N.Y.: Telegraph and Chronicle Press, 1866.

Rodenbough, Theo. F., and William L. Haskin, eds. *The Army of the United States: Historical Sketches of Staff and Line with Portraits of Generals-in-Chief.* New York: Maynard, Merrill, & Co., 1896.

Taylor, Richard. *Destruction and Reconstruction: Personal Experiences of the Civil War.* 1879. Rpt. with a new introduction by T. Michael Parrish. New York: Da Capo Press, 1995.

Transactions of the Southern Surgical and Gynecological Association. 28 vols. Birmingham, Ala.: Press of Caldwell Printing Co., 1887–1928.

Walker, J. G., and O. L. Shepherd. *The Navajo Reconnaissance: A Military Exploration of the Navajo Country in 1859.* Ed. L. R. Bailey. Los Angeles: Westernlore Press, 1964.

ARTICLES AND ESSAYS

Dimitry, John. "Louisiana." In Clement A. Evans, ed., *Confederate Military History* 10:3–312.

Fairbanks, Henry N. "The Red River Expedition of 1864." In *War Papers Read Before the Commandery of the State of Maine, Military Order of the Loyal Legion of the United States.* 4 vols. 1898–1915. Rpt. Wilmington, N. C.: Broadfoot, 1992. Vol. 1: 181–90.

Irwin, Richard B. "The Red River Campaign." In Johnson and Buel, eds., *Battles and Leaders* 4: 358–60.

Morton, Charles. "Third Regiment of Cavalry." In Rodenbough and Haskin, eds., *The Army of the United States,* 193–210.

Mulligan, James A. "The Siege of Lexington, Mo." In Johnson and Buel, eds., *Battles and Leaders* 1: 307–13.

Selfridge, Thomas O. "The Navy in the Red River." In Johnson and Buel, eds., *Battles and Leaders* 4: 362–66.

Smith, E. Kirby. "The Defense of Red River." In Johnson and Buel, eds., *Battles and Leaders* 4: 370–72.

Walker, John G. "Jackson's Capture of Harper's Ferry." In Johnson and Buel, eds., *Battles and Leaders* 2: 604–11.

Secondary Sources

BOOKS

Allardice, Bruce S. *More Generals in Gray.* Baton Rouge: Louisiana State University Press, 1995.

Arceneaux, William. *Acadian General Alfred Mouton and the Civil War.* 2nd ed. Lafayette: Center for Louisiana Studies, 1981.

Ballard, Michael B. *Vicksburg: The Campaign That Opened the Mississippi.* Chapel Hill: University of North Carolina Press, 2004.

Bearss, Edwin Cole. *The Campaign for Vicksburg.* 3 vols. Dayton, Ohio: Morningside House, 1985–86.

Bearss, Edwin C. *Steele's Retreat from Camden and the Battle of Jenkins' Ferry.* Little Rock: Arkansas Civil War Centennial Commission, 1967.

Bergeron, Arthur W., Jr. *Guide to Louisiana Confederate Military Units, 1861–1865.* Baton Rouge: Louisiana State University Press, 1989.

Black, Robert C. *The Railroads of the Confederacy.* Chapel Hill: University of North Carolina Press, 1952.

Boatner, Mark Mayo, III. *The Civil War Dictionary.* Rev. ed. New York: David McKay Co., 1988.

Carter, Arthur B. *Tarnished Cavalier: Major General Earl Van Dorn.* Knoxville: University of Tennessee Press, 1999.

Castel, Albert. *General Sterling Price and the Civil War in the West.* Baton Rouge: Louisiana State University Press, 1968.

Chaffin, Tom. *Pathfinder: John Charles Frémont and the Course of American Empire.* New York: Hill and Wang, 2002.

Christ, Mark K., ed. *Rugged and Sublime: The Civil War in Arkansas.* Fayetteville: University of Arkansas Press, 1994.

Connelly, Donald B. *John M. Schofield and the Politics of Generalship.* Chapel Hill: University of North Carolina Press, 2006.

Cotham, Edward T., Jr. *Battle on the Bay: The Civil War Struggle for Galveston.* Austin: University of Texas Press, 1998.

———. *Sabine Pass: The Confederacy's Thermopylae.* Austin: University of Texas Press, 2004.

Crute, Joseph H., Jr. *Units of the Confederate States Army.* Midlothian, Va.: Derwent Books, 1987.

Cunningham, Frank. *General Stand Watie's Confederate Indians.* Norman: University of Oklahoma Press, 1998.

Current, Richard N., ed. *Encyclopedia of the Confederacy.* 4 vols. New York: Simon & Schuster, 1993.

Cutrer, Thomas W. *Ben McCulloch and the Frontier Military Tradition.* Chapel Hill: University of North Carolina Press, 1993.

Daddysman, James W. *The Matamoros Trade: Confederate Commerce, Diplomacy, and Intrigue.* Newark: University of Delaware Press, 1984.

Davis, William C., ed. *The Confederate General.* 6 vols. Harrisburg, Pa.: National Historical Society, 1991.

DeBlack, Thomas A. *With Fire and Sword: Arkansas, 1861–1874.* Fayetteville: University of Arkansas Press, 2003.

Dufour, Charles L. *The Night the War Was Lost.* Garden City, N.Y.: Doubleday & Co., 1960.

Edmonds, David C. *Yankee Autumn in Acadiana: A Narrative of the Great Texas Overland Expedition through Southwestern Louisiana.* Lafayette, La.: Acadiana Press, 1979.

Engle, Stephen D. *Yankee Dutchman: The Life of Franz Sigel.* Baton Rouge: Louisiana State University Press, 1999.

Faulk, Odie B. *General Tom Green, Fightin' Texan.* Waco, Texas: Texian Press, 1963.

Faust, Patricia L., ed. *Historical Times Illustrated Encyclopedia of the Civil War.* New York: Harper & Row, Publishers, 1986.

Freeman, Douglas Southall. *Lee's Lieutenants: A Study in Command.* 3 vols. New York: C. Scribner's Sons, 1942–44.

Gerteis, Louis S. *Civil War St. Louis.* Lawrence: University Press of Kansas, 2001.

Hearn, Chester G. *Admiral David Dixon Porter.* Annapolis, Md.: Naval Institute Press, 1996.

Heidler, David S. and Jeanne T., eds. *Encyclopedia of the American Civil War: A Political, Social, and Military History.* New York: W. W. Norton & Co., 2000.

Hewitt, Lawrence Lee. *Port Hudson, Confederate Bastion on the Mississippi.* Baton Rouge: Louisiana State University Press, 1987.

History of Texas Together with a Biographical History of Tarrant and Parker Counties. Chicago: Lewis Publishing Co., 1895.

Hollandsworth, James G., Jr. *Pretense of Glory: The Life of General Nathaniel P. Banks.* Baton Rouge: Louisiana State University Press, 1998.

Johansson, M. Jane. *Peculiar Honor: A History of the 28th Texas Cavalry, 1862–1865.* Fayetteville: University of Arkansas Press, 1998.

Johnson, Ludwell. *Red River Campaign: Politics and Cotton in the Civil War.* Baltimore: Johns Hopkins Press, 1958.

Joiner, Gary Dillard. *One Damn Blunder from Beginning to End: The Red River Campaign of 1864.* Wilmington, Del.: Scholarly Resources, 2003.

Kerby, Robert L. *Kirby Smith's Confederacy: The Trans-Mississippi South, 1863–1865.* New York: Columbia University Press, 1972.

Kinard, Jeff. *Lafayette of the South: Prince Camille de Polignac and the American Civil War.* College Station: Texas A&M University Press, 2001.

King, James T. *War Eagle: A Life of General Eugene A. Carr.* Lincoln: University of Nebraska Press, 1963.

Kiper, Richard L. *Major General John Alexander McClernand: Politician in Uniform.* Kent, Ohio: Kent State University Press, 1999.

Kneebone, John T., J. Jefferson Looney, Brent Tarter, and Sandra Gioia Treadway, eds. *Dictionary of Virginia Biography.* 3 vols. to date. Richmond: Library of Virginia, 1998–.

Lamar, Howard R., ed. *The New Encyclopedia of the American West.* New Haven, Conn.: Yale University Press, 1998.

Lowe, Richard. *The Texas Overland Expedition of 1863.* 1996. Rpt. Abilene, Texas: McWhiney Foundation Press, 1998.

———. *Walker's Texas Division, C.S.A.: Greyhounds of the Trans-Mississippi.* Baton Rouge: Louisiana State University Press, 2004.

McCaslin, Richard B. *Fighting Stock: John S. "Rip" Ford of Texas.* Fort Worth, Texas: TCU Press, 2011.

McGowen, Stanley S. *Horse Sweat and Powder Smoke: The First Texas Cavalry in the Civil War.* College Station: Texas A&M University Press, 1999.

McPherson, James M. *Battle Cry of Freedom: The Civil War Era.* New York: Oxford University Press, 1988.

McReynolds, Edwin C. *Missouri: A History of the Crossroads State.* Norman: University of Oklahoma Press, 1962.

Mayeux, Steven M. *Earthen Walls, Iron Men: Fort DeRussy, Louisiana, and the Defense of Red River.* Knoxville: University of Tennessee Press, 2007.

Miller, Edward A. *Lincoln's Abolitionist General: The Biography of David Hunter.* Columbia: University of South Carolina Press, 1997.

Neal, Diane, and Thomas W. Kremm. *Lion of the South: General Thomas C. Hindman.* Macon, Ga.: Mercer University Press, 1993.

Parks, Joseph Howard. *General Edmund Kirby Smith, C.S.A.* Baton Rouge: Louisiana State University Press, 1954.

Parrish, T. Michael. *Richard Taylor: Soldier Prince of Dixie.* Chapel Hill: University of North Carolina Press, 1992.

Parrish, William E. *Turbulent Partnership: Missouri and the Union, 1861–1865.* Columbia: University of Missouri Press, 1963.

Phillips, Christopher. *Damned Yankee: The Life of General Nathaniel Lyon.* Columbia: University of Missouri Press, 1990.

Piston, William Garrett, and Richard W. Hatcher III. *Wilson's Creek: The Second Battle of the Civil War and the Men Who Fought It.* Chapel Hill: University of North Carolina Press, 2000.

Prushankin, Jeffery S. *A Crisis in Confederate Command: Edmund Kirby Smith, Richard Taylor, and the Army of the Trans-Mississippi.* Baton Rouge: Louisiana State University Press, 2005.

Robertson, James I., Jr. *Stonewall Jackson: The Man, the Soldier, the Legend.* New York: Macmillan Publishing, 1997.

Sears, Stephen W. *Landscape Turned Red: The Battle of Antietam.* New York: Ticknor & Fields, 1983.

Settles, Thomas M. *John Bankhead Magruder: A Military Reappraisal.* Baton Rouge: Louisiana State University, 2009.

Shalhope, Robert E. *Sterling Price: Portrait of a Southerner.* Columbia: University of Missouri Press, 1971.

Shea, William L. *Fields of Blood: The Prairie Grove Campaign.* Chapel Hill: University of North Carolina Press, 2009.

Shea, William L., and Earl J. Hess. *Pea Ridge: Civil War Campaign in the West.* Chapel Hill: University of North Carolina Press, 1992.

Silverstone, Paul H. *Warships of the Civil War Navies.* Annapolis, Md.: Naval Institute Press, 1989.

Smith, David Paul. *Frontier Defense in the Civil War: Texas' Rangers and Rebels.* College Station: Texas A&M University Press, 1992.

Smith, John David, ed. *Black Soldiers in Blue: African American Troops in the Civil War Era.* Chapel Hill: University of North Carolina Press, 2002.

Smith, Thomas T. *The Old Army in Texas: A Research Guide to the U.S.*

Army in Nineteenth-Century Texas. Austin: Texas State Historical Assn., 2000.

Smith, Thomas Tyree. *Fort Inge: Sharps, Spurs, and Sabers on the Texas Frontier, 1849–1869.* Austin, Texas: Eakin Press, 1993.

Snell, Mark. *From First to Last: The Life of William B. Franklin.* Bronx, N.Y.: Fordham University Press, 2002.

Symonds, Craig L. *Joseph E. Johnston: A Civil War Biography.* New York: W. W. Norton & Co., 1992.

Tanner, Robert G. *Stonewall in the Valley: Thomas J. "Stonewall" Jackson's Shenandoah Valley Campaign, Spring 1862.* Garden City, N.Y.: Doubleday & Co., 1976.

Townsend, Stephen A. *The Yankee Invasion of Texas.* College Station: Texas A&M University Press, 2006.

Trefousse, Hans L. *Ben Butler: The South Called Him Beast.* New York: Twayne Publishers, 1957.

Trudeau, Noah Andre. *Like Men of War: Black Troops in the Civil War, 1862–1865.* Boston: Little, Brown and Co., 1998.

Tyler, Ron, et al., eds. *The New Handbook of Texas.* 6 vols. Austin: Texas State Historical Assn., 1996.

Utley, Robert M. *Frontiersmen in Blue: The United States Army and the Indian, 1848–1865.* New York: Macmillan Publishing Co., 1967.

Warner, Ezra J. *Generals in Blue: Lives of the Union Commanders.* Baton Rouge: Louisiana State University Press, 1964.

———. *Generals in Gray: Lives of the Confederate Commanders.* Baton Rouge: Louisiana State University Press, 1959.

Winters, John D. *The Civil War in Louisiana.* Baton Rouge: Louisiana State University Press, 1963.

Wise, Stephen R. *Lifeline of the Confederacy: Blockade Running During the Civil War.* Columbia: University of South Carolina Press, 1988.

Wooster, Ralph A. *Texas and Texans in the Civil War.* Austin, Texas: Eakin Press, 1995.

ARTICLES AND ESSAYS

Bailey, Anne J. "Was There a Massacre at Poison Spring?" *Military History of the Southwest* 20 (Fall 1990): 157–68.

Bearss, Edwin C. "The Battle of Helena, July 4, 1863." *Arkansas Historical Quarterly* 20 (Autumn 1961): 256–97.

Clampitt, Brad R. "The Breakup: The Collapse of the Confederate Trans-Mississippi Army in Texas, 1865." *Southwestern Historical Quarterly* 108 (April 2005): 498–534.

Crisler, Robert M. "Missouri's Little Dixie." *Missouri Historical Review* 42 (January 1948): 130–39.

DeBlack, Thomas A. "1863: 'We Must Stand or Fall Alone.'" In Christ, ed., *Rugged and Sublime,* 59–103.

Gentry, Judith F. "White Gold: The Confederate Government and Cotton in Louisiana." *Louisiana History* 33 (Spring 1992): 229–40.

Hewitt, Lawrence Lee. "An Ironic Route to Glory: Louisiana's Native Guards at Port Hudson." In Smith, ed., *Black Soldiers in Blue,* 78–106.

Joiner, Gary D., and Charles E. Vetter. "The Union Naval Expedition on the Red River, March 12–May 22, 1864." *Civil War Regiments* 4 (no. 2, 1994): 26–67.

Lowe, Richard. "Battle on the Levee: The Fight at Milliken's Bend, Louisiana." In Smith, ed., *Black Soldiers in Blue,* 107–35.

Michot, Stephen S. "In Relief of Port Hudson: Richard Taylor's 1863 Lafourche Offensive." *Military History of the West* 23 (Fall 1993): 103–34.

Roberts, Bobby. "Rivers of No Return." In *"The Earth Reeled and Trees Trembled": Civil War Arkansas, 1863–1864,* ed. Mark Christ (Old State House Museum, 2007), 74–88.

Shea, William L. "1862: 'A Continual Thunder.'" In Christ, ed., *Rugged and Sublime,* 21–58.

Sutherland, Daniel E. "1864: 'A Strange, Wild Time.'" In Christ, ed. *Rugged and Sublime,* 105–44.

Vandiver, Frank E. "Texas and the Confederate Army's Meat Problem." *Southwestern Historical Quarterly* 47 (January 1944): 225–33.

WORLD WIDE WEB

Battle of Lexington [Missouri] State Historic Site. www.mostateparks .com/lexington/battle.htm

Jenkins' Ferry [Arkansas] State Park. www.arkansasstateparks.com/ jenkinsferry/

Mansfield State Historic Site. www.crt.state.la.us/parks/imansfld.aspx

Index